Tortilla Soup for the Spirit

Ellen Castro
And
Betty Ramirez Swinners

Outskirts Press, Inc.
Denver, Colorado

Tortilla Soup For the Spirit
All Rights Reserved
Copyright © 2006 Betty Ramirez Swinners and Ellen Castro

Outskirts Press
http://www.outskirtspress.com

ISBN 10: 1-59800-211-2
ISBN 13: 978-1-59800-211-9

A Word from the Authors

Welcome to this delicious collection of work written by Latinas and Latinos from across the country. The compilation reflects the many aspects of our heritage and culture, including our deep faith and love for life.

Also, many, many thanks to the contributors for sharing their hearts and thoughts. We thank God for our families, friends and many blessings...for God is full of miracles.

From our hearts to yours, may faith, hope and love abound.

Enjoy!

Ellen and Betty

Table of Contents

Cultural y Recuerdos

Cultura y Recuerdos

Culture and Memories

Everything about our culture includes a deep faith, a love for life and family, and our total enjoyment of food. It is embedded in our very being, and seeks to be celebrated and enjoyed. Our culture is our heritage. It is a heritage of survival and strength, of deep belief in God, and of richness and beauty.

This culture makes us very sentimental people. We feel deeply, and cherish our memories of loved ones and experiences. Our recuerdos are woven into a rich tapestry of feelings that bring peace, comfort and gratitude to our hearts.

Reflections in Los Cabos

Ellen Castro

As I sit on the beach looking at the beautiful, expansive ocean, drinking my Modelo, I thank God for my heritage, but it hasn't always been so.

While attending a Caucasian high school, as well as being only one of eight Mexican Americans at Southern Methodist University in Dallas, I just wanted to "fit in." Of course when asked, I would proudly tell people that I was Mexican. But trust me, in subtle and not so subtle ways, I denied my culture. God knows...no tanning for me then.

Yet today, I thank God, the Mother Mary, and Jesus Christ for my heritage, olive skin, big brown eyes and my warmth. Warmth describes our culture.

Warmth. Love. Kindness. Gentleness. Tenderness. Those are not the words that describe my American side, which is driven, efficient, and hard to the core, based on over twenty years in a male-dominated business world. No wonder, for many years, I have had to struggle from within to deny my warmth and tenderness. The chasm.

Being Mexican, I shudder at the thought of "manana." And yet with the attitude of "manana" comes the joy of accepting what is important today...enjoying the moment...enjoying life. It is not a constant striving to be thinner, richer, or more successful. It is resting when tired and accepting God's grace. Valuing family and love.

I believe in thanking God, not cursing Him. It is Primero Dios...a belief in faith and service...acceptance of one's plan in life. It is my place as Mexican and American.

Ah...the Mexicana who loves vibrant colors versus pastels. Spicy food versus bland. Ah...the woman who sees God in the littlest creature, in a flower, in an ocean, in everyone. Ah...the woman who does the sign of the cross in reverence, faith and awe. The Mexicana who has native intelligence and creativity...loves mariachis and dancing salsa.

Gracias a Dios, for I finally love and accept all of me.

Dichos... My Interpretation

Betty Swinners

Dichos are phrases meant to reach your heart and soul with just a few words. There have been many times in my life when I've had to make decisions using a dicho to compare my circumstances at the time. Here are a few of my favorites.

"No hay mal que por bien no venga." Nothing bad ever happens that something good does not come out of it. How many times has a family emergency brought unity to a family? How about when you lost a "good job?" Didn't a better one come along? When your heart was broken, did you fall in love again? I believe everything happens for a reason and have found it to be true for me.

"Aunque la mona se vista de seda, no deja de ser mona." Even if the doll wears silk, she is still a doll. To me this means many things. It doesn't matter how you try to disguise yourself, you will still be the same person. If you are being abused, it doesn't matter what beautiful silk dress they buy you to wear, you will still be a battered woman.

"Aunque la jaula sea de oro, no deja de ser prision." Even if the cage is made of gold, it is still a prison. How true this is! I had what I thought was my "big break." I had an executive office with a beautiful window overlooking an atrium, and was making a six-figure income. The guy I worked for was very abusive and controlling. He once said these words: "Betty, understand that you will make a lot of money when I let you, without me you will never succeed." He knew I was a strong woman and he made it a point in his daily routine to make me cry. I quit my six-figure job and took the first job I could find. It paid $500 a month. Now I own my own business and have never been happier. I am going to make a lot of money...without him.

"Cuando una puerta se ciera, Dios abre una ventana." When someone closes a door, God opens a window. Always have faith. There is always a solution and a way out. When you feel the world is closing in and you run into dead ends, take a moment and look for the window that God has opened for you, like He has for me.

"Mejor sola que mal acompanada." You are better off alone than with bad company. Don't underestimate yourself. If someone doesn't want to go somewhere with you, you should go alone and have a great time. Don't live with someone who does not enjoy your company, or that will make your life miserable. You are better off alone and will be much happier. Believe in yourself!

"No hay borracho que coma lumbre." There is not a drunk that will eat fire. I have found people who drink and know their behavior prior to getting drunk. They act out and blame the booze for their actions. This saying makes sense. Try lighting a flame and asking a drunken person to eat it. It won't happen. Remember this saying when someone tells you, "I didn't know what I was doing; I was drunk." The truth is the alcohol just gave them the courage to do it.

Salsa, The Ultimate Weapon

Raoul Lowery Contreras

It's a dance! It's a weapon! It's a vegetable! It is salsa. Yes, the Meso-American gift to the culinary world, the one made from tomatoes, chiles, onions and other "exotic" ingredients, was declared a vegetable by the Department of Agriculture.

In the early 1980's, the Department of Agriculture, under Ronald Regan's presidency, tried to label ketchup a vegetable for school lunch programs, just as the Clinton administration did with salsa. Looking at a ketchup label, I find the only difference in ingredients between ketchup and salsa, is that ketchup doesn't have chile and does contain corn syrup.

Despite these tiny differences, the Reagan administration was keel-hauled and lambasted all over the map by the American liberal, educational and child-protection establishments. Criminal was but one of the milder epithets hurled at what the disgraced, former Democrat mucky-muck, Clark Clifford, referred to as "the amiable dunce" – Ronald Reagan to those outside the Washington Beltway. The furor lasted and lasted. The turmoil was silly then, and the proof is this very salsa anointment.

All that aside, salsa is more than a vegetable, it is a weapon. It is perhaps the most devastating weapon in the war to retake America for the Hispanics, the original European owners of more than three-quarters of what is now the United States. Guns, missiles, tanks and grenades are useless in this war, which is the Reconquest, la Reconquista of the lost territories. The continuing and growing popularity and acceptance of salsa is essential to the plans of the conspirators of the Reconquista.

First, came the massive marketing campaign to make salsa a bigger seller than ketchup. Bingo! The profits of salsa are now being used to finance the Reconquista. Also, the federal government now officially recognizes salsa. Thankfully, the takeover is progressing nicely, and is happening with the full cooperation of Washington bureaucrats. Holy enchilada!

Food, you see, is a weapon. This is especially true when one speaks of tasty, wholesome, healthy, spicy Mexican food. Ah...what a weapon: tacos, enchiladas, tamales, beans, rice, burritos, chimichangas...What? Oh, I forgot. Burritos and chimichangas aren't well known south of the great Mexican Desert. Those little Indians of southern Mexico don't know what these things are, nor are they conversant with tortillas made from flour. No, these northern Mexican and desert-born gourmet items are native to the north, and to the former Mexican territories of Texas, New Mexico and California (aka Aztlan).

Yes! These very territories are being retaken by the onslaught of salsa and jalapenos. Next, we'll see McTacos and McBurritos with McSalsa, and maybe we'll see double enchiladas with cheese and stuffed-with-Jack cheese jalapenos. There will be taco stands with drive-through windows, walk-in taco shacks, and converted, failed hamburger stands painted with orange and yellow paint, named with some variation of Robertos, Hilbertos, Albertos, Adalbertos, etc.

There will be fancy, sit down restaurants. They will have the ever-present ubiquitous salsa. The converts and the very addicted, who will turn the country over to the Reconquistas, will eat it. Salsa, like most Mexican food, is addictive. Who can deny the delights of a chicken enchilada smothered with sour cream, guacamole (wah-kah-moh-leh) and salsa? Who?

Oh, the reader doesn't know what guacamole is? Well, it is the greatest gift from God that can be thought of by a human being. A ripe avocado, crushed garlic, chopped tomatoes and onions, chopped cilantro, lime or lemon juice and, my favorite, chopped pine nuts, all mixed together into a soft, butter-like consistency. Having originated in ancient Mexico, the avocado and its ultimate concoction, guacamole, is a weapon, and also in the Reconquista. It is second only to salsa.

Yes, salsa is the weapon. In September it will be in almost every school where there is a lunch program. Each child will now be addicted to salsa. Then they will become warriors of the Reconquista, too. Chuckle, little blonde, blue-eyed kids selling out their parents and country because of salsa. Wow! What will the patriotic, militia-types do now? The federal government has turned on them and sold out. Their children will turn on them and sell out. People who like great food will turn on them and sell out. The patriotic, militia-types will be left alone, twisting, slowly twisting in the wind, subsisting on non-vegetable ketchup, the number two seller behind number one salsa.

Victory, the Reconquista of the lost territories, the Hispanization of the United States of America by hot sauce, by salsa, the accompanying guacamole and other Mexican food. What a delicious thought.

Juan Gonzalez

Elpidio Brambilla Castro, Jr.

Juan Gonzalez was born in 1835 and died in San Antonio in 1922, at the age of eighty-seven. He was a native of Mexico...Bustamente, Nuevo Leon to be exact. While he was not a rich man, he was a gentleman of means. At that time, he was head of a household that included two daughters, Margarita and Enriquetta, plus Margarita's children named Eloisa, Arturo and Delia.

It was during the time of the revolution in Mexico, and Arturo, the middle son in his early twenties, was the town's telegraph operator. While the government employed Arturo, the Revolutionaries wanted him also. You see, at that time the best means of communication was the telegraph.

Word reached the family that the Revolutionaries were either going to kidnap Arturo or have him shot. This prompted Don Juan to sell whatever he owned—land, home and furnishings—to a neighbor, and head north. Needless to say, nothing was ever recovered.

Upon arriving in Laredo, Mexico and waiting for immigration, the youngest child, Delia, was reading a book to her grandfather. A photographer happened to come by and was impressed by the beauty of the lovely child reading to the elegant old man to keep him occupied, so he took a picture. Amazingly, another relative coming to the States saw the photograph in the photographer's shop window and recognized the subjects. By a miracle, they bought the picture and gave it to the family.

At the immigration office, everything went fine and everyone was clear to enter the United States, with the exception of this old man. At his age, immigration authorities decided he would be a liability and imposition to the U.S. as an old refugee. Thus, he was refused admission to the Promised Land and returned to Mexico.

Eloisa, the oldest, and my mother, stayed and took care of him in Laredo while waiting for arrangements to get across as "mojodos," or illegal aliens. After waiting for some time, word came that all was arranged to get them across the Rio Grande into Texas. They crossed in a "lancha" canoe, but at landing time it toppled over, sending all into the cold water. Obviously all survived and were taken to San Antonio by car. Sadly and ironically, "Don Juanito" caught pneumonia and died within a month, but with the happy realization that he had brought his immediate family to safety.

Viva "El Espirita de Sobrevivir" y de mi parte, gracias for being born in this country, U.S.A. To this day, Aunt Delia Davila recounts this bittersweet story to whoever will listen and me. And of course, she shows the beautiful picture of her and Don Juanito, which is displayed in her apartment at the nursing home where she now lives. The photograph is also displayed affectionately and proudly at the homes of her four children, my home, the homes of my two daughters, Eloise and Ellen, and my grandson, Allen.

Chile y Tomate

Betty Swinners

So many luncheons, dinners and conferences to go to and everywhere I went, I looked for brown people like me. Nowhere could I find one. Oh wait...I think I see one! Nope. It was a white person with a tan. *Where is my Raza?* I wondered. Surely some made it out of the barrio, too.

The very first time I went to a high profile, Hispanic banquet I was so excited. Latinas! I walked in and said to a few smiling faces, "Que paso?" I felt like a stranger among my own people. The food was awful! It was the same kind of food that was served at the "other" luncheons. No spices, tortillas, guacamole or salsa. Nothing. This was not what I expected.

No one wanted to speak Spanish to me. Eventually I went and sat at a table with some "friendly" faces. I am a really funny person, so I've been told, so to start conversation at my table I asked, "Where is the chile y tomate?"

One of the women at the table, named Delia, opened her purse and pulled out some small serrano chiles and some little salad tomatoes. "Aqui estan, comele." (*Eat up*)

That impacted me. I learned from Delia something very important, which is to take pride in who you are and your culture. More times than not we have to bury our cultura in order to survive in mainstream communities. And when we are among other Latinas, our culture is so buried that we cannot even share it with each other.

I thank God for my accomplishments. I am an entrepreneur in an executive's world, spending most of my time in boardrooms, living in the suburbs, driving a minivan and, let's not forget, the many luncheons, dinners and conferences. However everywhere I go, I look for brown people like me. I may be out of the barrio, but the barrio is still in me.

Mothers Know Best

Eddie Reyes

In 1962, when I was twelve years old. My father accidentally drowned while swimming during a family picnic on Mother's Day. At the time, I was attending Sacred Heart Catholic School.

Father Gene, my alter boy instructor and schoolteacher, helped my mother throughout the entire funeral and burial process. After being informed by my mother that I was now the "man of the house," I felt it was my duty to somehow repay Father Gene for his help. One day I asked him if he had one wish, what would it be? He quickly told me that he had always hoped that one of us altar boys would become a priest. With this in mind, I approached him a few days later saying that I had dreamed I was a priest.

He quickly became overwhelmed with pride and joy. Eventually, I ended up in a seminary and I instantly knew that this was not what I wanted to do for the rest of my life! I was miserable, homesick and overwhelmed. The seminary was like boot camp – extremely strict, complete silence, academically challenging, and with long hours.

In my second week, my older cousins snuck me out one night and got me completely inebriated. During the predawn hours, they returned me to the seminary and left me sleeping on the stairs of the rectory! I was awakened by the headmaster priest and after having to say two hours worth of penance, I met with the headmaster. The headmaster instructed me to have my mother come pick me up. It was obvious that the priesthood was not my calling.

With great reluctance and embarrassment, I forced myself to phone my mom. As I was dialing, I envisioned that I was going to break her heart, that I would cause her to be extremely disappointed, and that I had brought shame upon our home and family name. To my surprise, she was completely nonchalant about it and expressed great relief to hear that I was coming home. Mothers can sense things about their children that no one else can. She ended our conversation by stating the following, "No te preocupes mi 'hito, ya se que fuistes al seminario para estudiar para hacer Papa, pero saliste Camote!"

Comfort Food Flashbacks

Minerva Gorena, Ed.D.

"*Round, flat, circles patted out by hand, cooked on heated griddles, staples of the land. Filled with savories such as meat or eggs or tasty beans, tortillitas sabrocitas, food stuff made for queens!*"

It's a quiet summer evening, and I'm standing in my kitchen where I've just finished preparing my dinner. Turning to open the refrigerator door, I reach inside and take out a plastic package of my favorite comfort food, corn tortillas. Opening the package, I place four of the tortillas in the toaster oven to heat. As I wait for the toaster to do its job, memories of days gone by come flooding back. Oh, how life has changed, and I lament over what was and what will never be again.

As I wrap the heated tortillas in aluminum foil, organize my tray, walk down the steps to the basement to sit down to a solitary meal, I reflect and reminisce as my comfort food flashbacks fill my mind. I begin to think how unfortunate it is that my niece and nephews will never have the kinds of experiences I had with corn tortillas.

Flashback! There's my maternal grandmother and there I am, as young as four. We're walking together, my hand in hers. The neighborhood is familiar as we walk the three or four blocks to the "tortillera." Familiar faces extend greetings as we walk by Dona Sarita's house, Tia Merced's, and by the little corner neighborhood "tiendita." There we go, grandmother and granddaughter, holding hands, admiring the bright flowers in the many gardens along the way, avoiding barking dogs and enjoying the cool peaceful morning.

Even before we arrive, we see other ladies and children going in and out of the small building located right in the middle of the block, la tortilleria. There's no grass and no sidewalk, but it's where the fresh hand-made tortillas are available daily from dawn to one or two o'clock in the afternoon. When we enter, there are the familiar greetings from the ladies and children waiting for their orders, and from the ladies, las tortilleras, standing behind the counter. There's the owner, of course, busily cutting sheets of white butcher paper and placing from five to twenty-five hot corn tortillas in the center of each sheet of paper. Then he is folding the paper around the stack to form a neat package that I could never seem to replicate. As I reflect, I think how amazing it was during the late 1940's and early 1950's. Those tortillas cost only a penny a piece! How many tortillas did the owner have to sell to make a profit?

There they are, four or five tortilleras, patting out by hand those perfectly round tortillas and then placing them on the square, or rectangular, metal griddle that occupied the center of the small room. There they stood, each one at attention, at their special stations. Each one waiting for her mound of freshly ground corn masa to be placed on the black lava rock metate by their side. It was fascinating to watch the synchronized actions that each tortillera performed in making each one of the tortillas.

As they chatted with one another, or exchanged greetings with customers, they would dip their hands into a water container, pat the mound of fresh masa on the metate, and pick up the black, lava rock "rolling pin-type implement," referred to as "la mano" del metate. With "la mano" del metate, they would knead the fresh masa by moving it back and forth until a smaller mound was formed that they could work with. Another dip of the hands into the water, a scoop of masa, and the patting would begin again.

How'd they do that? To me it was like magic to watch those hands automatically pat and turn, pat and turn, and then form those perfect, round circles in what seemed like seconds. The rhythmic patting as they all worked together was also a mystery to me. How could they stand there, laughing, talking, patting and hardly looking at their hands while they created those perfect circles? And then, with the flash of a hand, they'd place those circles on the hot griddle to cook. How'd they do it? With one hand they'd place the finished tortilla on the griddle, then just as quickly flip over those that were cooking or flip them into a dishtowel-lined box. And then they'd start all over again – knead, knead, form a ball, pat, pat, pat, flip, cook...

The owner would walk around to where each of the tortilleras stood, check their boxes and count out the tortillas to fill the orders placed by the customers. As we waited for our order to be filled, my grandmother would chat with other customers in conversational exchanges related to the weather, illness in the neighborhood, births, deaths, and who was going where and when, how much I had grown, how long I'd be staying with her, and how the other grandchildren were doing.

There was always that warm, wonderful feeling of community, of caring, of interest and concern for one another that was both welcoming and comforting. As I recall, we'd always take home two packages, one filled with hot tortillas and the other of freshly ground, raw corn masa. On our walk back to my grandparent's home, I'd always ask for a little ball of the raw masa and when I'd finished eating it, I'd ask for a piece of a hot tortilla. Once back home, my grandmother would give me some tortillas with my meals and would use the raw masa to make "gorditas" – small thick tortillas made by mixing bacon or pork cracklings with drippings and salt. Those "gorditas" were considered special treats and were always wonderful! The tortillera was a part of our lives in South Texas. Although white bread from the grocery store was good, and my Mama made flour tortillas, those corn tortillas were, and still are, my favorites!

Another flashback! It's a Sunday! Church services are over and there's the traditional stop at the tortilleria right next to the church. I'd join my uncle and his family in their car for a short ride to my house and out would come the saltshaker from the glove compartment! We all had to have our Sunday morning "corn tortilla fix" before we got home! The package of tortillas would be opened and my Aunt would hand one to each of us so that we could sprinkle on a little salt, roll it up, and savor each bite. They would drop me off at my house, just a short block away. As I waved goodbye, armed with my favorite comfort food, off they would go, waving their hot, rolled corn tortillas at me as they drove to their home for Sunday dinner. Those were the days!

As I continue to reflect, I realize that it wasn't until years later that I actually thought about, or was curious about, those early women entrepreneurs that owned those little tortilla factories. It was a revelation to learn the time-consuming process they followed so that I could have my corn tortillas. Starting the day before, they'd boil whole, dry corn kernels in special tubs and then let them cool off until early the next morning. The cooked corn kernels were then drained and placed in special electric, metal "molinos" that would grind the corn to make the masa. The owners and their assistants would begin their days at five o'clock each morning so that they were ready to greet customers at 6:00 a.m. South Texas is hot, and those women would stand, day-in-day-out, in front of those hot gas griddles with little or no ventilation as they made hundreds of tortillas.

Oh, how times have changed! Today thousands of tortillas are made daily across the country. We read of tortilla barons making millions from the sale of packaged corn masa products. There are chips, taco shells, and tortillas in all colors, such as blue corn, yellow corn, white corn and even red chili. And there are many flavors, such as nacho cheese, ranch, guacamole, garlic, lime – and list goes on. I wonder, as I eat my dinner accompanied, as usual, with my favorite tortillas, corn tortillas for the soul, if those pioneering tortilleras knew then what the future would be. And what would they say today?

Famosa Estrella

Veronica Guajardo

Modesto summers turn black asphalt roads to moving waves and ripples, like the water ripples at Marshall pool that's too far to walk to and costs too much to get in.

Ni modo, so Chata and I go inside to watch TV and drink sweet, purple Kool-Aid with ice cubes, in plastic jumbo cups. Then Chata calls Rey *su novio* on the phone. They're both thirteen, but it's still true love at first sight. *"Por vida,"* she says.

She tells him how much she misses him, and he promises to come over after work. He works at the Rocket Tire Shop that's in front of National Market at "Four Corners." This is where they first met when she was buying her favorite after-school *chulchulucos que es una, 32 oz. Pepsi* with extra ice, and a bag of saladitos con limon.

"Tonight, *mijo*?" she says, and is real excited 'til su *madre y Tia mia* comes in through the backdoor. Chata hangs up the phone real quick when she hears the screen door slam. I flip the channels and Chata smiles. "We're just watching TV, Tia," I say.

Then Tia yells at Chata for not doing her *que haceres,* "*que nina floja!*" "No one will marry a lazy girl," she says. So Chata quickly begins to wash dishes and sweep the floors, the crumbs of tortilla and chicken bones under the table because her little brothers *son unos puercos para comer*. She just smiles and sweeps faster.

I see her cleaning and I know Chata and Rey will be together always and forever. "Each moment with you, it's just like a dream to me, that somehow came true," she sings and sings *toda la tarde.*

And I know Chata will soon push a stroller down the street, *por la calle Leon,* and she'll drop out, but come after school and everyone will come around her to see her new baby. I know we will become *mas y mas apartadas.* I'll miss her.

So maybe I'll have a baby too, to roll *juntas por la calle Leon,* together. Anyway, we're grownups now. But I need a boyfriend. I'm smart enough to know boyfriends make babies when they hold your hand, and make blue and purple marks all over your neck. Chata calls them chupetes, even though they look like bruises. But boys are gross! *Todititos todos.* Except one, *Pedrito Fernandez,* who sings *La Mochila Azul!* And he sings it to me *porque tengo los ojitos dormilones.* Maybe he'll be my *novio. Si? Sobres?* So, Pedrito and I are *novios.* I know he loves me because when we were little kids, we'd climb into the abandoned blue bus behind the housing project where we lived.

Mom called the projects *la vecindad,* because she said the neighbors knew all your chismes, *y que no se podia hechar uno un pedo sin que lo supiera el vecindario. Yo y la Chata* would climb into that rusty bus through the shattered glass of the front window and jump on the seats, rip the springs out and use them as bracelets, and knot the seat belts. I would sit on the steering wheel and try not to fall off while Chata turned it to shake me off. *Pero nel paster que no me caia porque,* I was too good! The air was thick and enclosed, twice as hot inside, but that was OK, *no le hace,* because we knew we were *famosas estrellas.*

We were *artistas, cantantes,* Mexican singers with shiny, short dresses and *y mucho* make-up. We were in that blue bus driving, on our way to *Siempre en Domingo con Raul Velazco,* where we would meet *los chicos guapos de Menudo, y claro, a mi me estaria esperando mi Pedrito Fernandez, quien me cantaria a mi,* because he was my boyfriend. We'd arrive to the studios in Mexico City, *a los foros de Televisa, S.A. de C.V., bien arregladitas y muy pintaditas,* and everyone would look and look and want a picture *con nosotras y con los chicos de Menudo y con mi Pedrito Fernandez.*

Nosotras por se tan famosas, los chicos de Menudo y Pedrito Fernandez, would be waiting there for us, eager to hold our hand, *por vida* always and forever each moment with you. It's just like a dream to me that somehow came true.

Tortillas ... Food of the Spirit

Ellen Castro

Wow, yum, ahh. Whenever I eat tortillas, I seem to connect to my softer side, my Mexican heritage. My heritage is of faith, family and carino. The aroma and texture bring me joy, whether in the diet version of corn or the delicious nature of flour.

I remember being ridiculed at my Anglo school for eating tacos for breakfast. Was I insane? I didn't act Mexican. Of course, I defended my heritage, my right to eat tortillas, and myself. It was humorous, yet sad. Oh well, in hindsight, I should have been sad for them...pobrecitos. The glorious tortilla. I still salivate when I think of them.

Tortillas are an awesome delicacy that can be served and eaten in so many ways. Tortillas can serve as spoons, forks, dippers, pancakes, etc. And of course you can eat them with your hands! What decadence! Tortillas can be eaten alone with salt or butter, or stuffed with meat, beans, cheese, vegetables, salsa, and guacamole to be tacos. Or they can be eaten as enchiladas. Or as pizzas. Your imagination is the only limit.

Thank God for my heritage. Thank God for tortillas. Tortillas are food for the soul or common cold. Tortillas...

Buen provecho!

Easter, A Day of Ham, Pineapple and Refried Beans

Raoul Lowery Contreras

When I was an eight-year-old boy, Easter Sunday meant three things to me: my mother bought a big white hat to wear to church; it always seemed to rain on Easter Sunday; and we always had a terrific ham baked under a blanket of pineapple rings. I don't know why we had ham on Easter Sunday and I don't know why we had pineapple rings either. It didn't matter why; it was a terrific dinner. The rain always bugged me, for it hardly rains at all in San Diego. So, why the rain on Easter Sunday? The reason was simple. On the greatest day of the Christian calendar, the day all life is renewed, the rain came because the buses hardly ran, and my mother and I had to walk four miles to and from Our Lady of Sacred Heart. Of course, it would rain on our mother and son parade.

The Easter of 1950 brought a stepfather from central Texas who knew ham, but pineapple was out of his universe. Not being a Roman Catholic didn't help him understand why it was so important for us to be at church on Easter Sunday, but then again, I didn't know either. Not speaking Latin didn't help. But the Irish priest managed to explain it to us, despite his brogue being so strong. Therefore, only half of the congregation, the English-speaking half, could barely understand him. At least we didn't have to walk to and from church anymore, I thought. Wrong! My stepfather, a rookie cop, had to work on Sundays, especially Easter Sundays. It rained that Easter. My mother's big white hat, almost as big as her umbrella, got a little wet. During mass, I prayed my mother would learn to drive before next Easter. She didn't. Easter of 1951 arrived on schedule with low-hanging, rain-filled clouds, and the driver of the house had to work again. My mother still didn't know how to drive. This time I had to push a stroller with my new brother all the way to church and back. Have you ever tried to push a stroller in a light rain and hold an umbrella at the same time?

Finally, in 1952, I was able to ride in a car to Easter service. It didn't rain that day. I still couldn't understand the priest. But after mass he pulled me aside and asked if I wanted to be an altar boy. Of course! Of course I wanted to be an altar boy. I figured I would be able to finally understand him, because he would have to speak to me in Latin and that was easier than my learning Irish. I had to be confirmed first, for a Catholic boy wasn't really Catholic until he was confirmed.

Confirmation classes were after school, so my days got longer and longer. I had to study my confirmation lesson book in school and on the bus on the way to class. There, I learned about Easter. The priest told me, "On the third day He arose from the dead and ascended to heaven." Really? I was eleven. Wow, I thought, that Jesus was really something; he had to be the Son of God, without a doubt.

No wonder Easter was the most important day of the year. The proof had to be that we had ham on that day; the only time we ever had ham. Ham cost a lot of money then, and it was a lot of money to us before my step dad joined the family with his $300-a-month, police officer's salary. It was very special. The day we had it, had to be a very special day.

By 1954, I had three younger brothers. When we went to church, mother dressed them all exactly the same, complete with bow ties. I didn't have to wear a bow tie, even on Easter. It was that 1954 Easter that we hosted the whole family. We had three hams that time. There must not have been a pineapple left in Hawaii. Everyone had such a good time that the family decided Easter dinner would be at our house the next year, and the year after that.

And so it went every year. A beautiful ham, pineapples, mashed potatoes, sweet potatoes, green beans, corn, refried beans, and Spanish rice made our Easter dinner. What? Refried beans and Spanish rice? Well, except for my step dad, we are Mexican, you know.

The Easter after I came home from the U.S. Marines is perhaps the most memorable of my life. I had re-enrolled in college and was working at a new Safeway grocery store in the city's first major shopping mall. The day before Easter, I went to work and was told by the smiling store manager to report to the mall office for a day's work. "OK," I said.

At the mall office, the pretty receptionist giggled when she saw me and then she called her boss. He laughed as he shook my hand and led me into his office. There it was, a large white, bunny rabbit suit, complete with ears that were almost two feet high. I stared at it. It was my size.

It was a great and happy Easter that year. The family dinner was a riot of laughter. After all, how many families could celebrate life's renewal and the Ascension with a real live, six-foot tall Easter Bunny in the family?

War, Death and Chocolate, Memorial Day, 1998

Raoul Lowery Contreras

The train from El Paso, Texas to Los Angeles was full of men in uniform. Sailors, soldiers and Marines, warriors all, were going to the Pacific to fight Imperial Japan. In November, 1943, the United States had been at war for nearly two years.

I was on that train. I spoke not a word of English. For, you see, I had just crossed the border from the country of my birth, Mexico, to live in the country of my citizenship, the United States of America, a country at war with the greatest of all evils. I didn't know any of this then, because I wasn't even three years old. What I did know was that warriors laughed and gave me chocolate when I made funny faces. Thus, using the impeccable logic of an almost three-year-old, I wandered throughout the train making funny faces and making warriors laugh. I was full of chocolate the entire trip.

HERRERA, SILVESTRE S., Private First Class, U.S. Army, near Mertwiller, France, 15 March 1945. Born-El Paso, Texas, Medal of Honor citation...he made a one-man frontal assault on a strongpoint and captured eight enemy soldiers. Pvt. Herrera again moved forward, disregarding the danger of exploding mines, to attack the position. He stepped on a mine and had both feet severed, but despite intense pain and unchecked loss of blood, he pinned down the enemy with accurate rifle fire.

"COMMIES INVADE SOUTH KOREA" was the newspaper headlines on June 25, 1950. I knew there was a war on that day, because my ice cream bar, that cost a nickel the day before, had doubled in price. At nine-and-a-half, I knew that war brought inflated prices; I remembered WWII ration coupons and higher prices right after the war.

OBREGAON, EUGENE ARNOLD, Private First Class, U.S. Marine Corps, Seoul, Korea, 26 September 1950. Born – Los Angeles, California. Medal of Honor citation – Pfc. Obregon observed a fellow Marine fall wounded. Armed only with a pistol, Pfc. Obregon dashed from his covered position to the side of the casualty. Firing his pistol with one hand as he ran, he grasped his comrade by the arm. With his other hand, Obregon dragged him to the side of the road, when hostile troops began advancing. Obregon placed his own body as a shield, and lay there firing accurately and effectively into the hostiles until he was fatally wounded.

I rode my bike past the little corner grocery store on the way to the fifth grade every morning. There, that morning, the newspaper headline screamed: "TRUMAN FIRES MACARTHUR." I turned and raced home to awake my father, screaming my first political statement, "That son-of-a-bitch Truman fired General MacArthur." President Truman had fired our Korean War commander.

My second political statement was my "I Like Ike" button in the eighth grade in 1952. Candidate General Eisenhower promised to "Go to Korea" to end the stalemated war. I knew he would; he did and he won.

My first day in college was four months before I turned eighteen. When that birthday came, I left the house for my eight o'clock class, like I did every day. I came home later than usual, just as my three younger brothers and parents sat for dinner. My mother, noticing a little extra gusto in me, asked, "How was your day?"

I replied, "Fine."

"Are you sure?" she asked.

"Yes, the day was very, very good."

"Why was it so good?" she asked.

"Because I joined the Marines today."

JIMENEZ, JOSE FRANCISCO, Lance Corporal, U.S. Marines Corps, Quang Nam Province, Vietnam, 28 August 1969. Born – Mexico City, Federal District, Mexico. Medal of Honor citation – L/Cpl Jimenez reacted by seizing the initiative and plunging forward toward the enemy positions. He personally destroyed several enemy personnel and silenced an anti-aircraft weapon. He slowly maneuvered to within ten feet of hostile soldiers who were firing automatic weapons. In the face of vicious enemy fire, he destroyed the position and continued to press forward until he was mortally wounded.

All three of my drill instructors fought in the Korean War that ended just six years before the day I walked into Marine boot camp. They survived. Thirty-three thousand, six hundred and twenty-nine American were killed and 8,000 more were missing in Korea. Many of my boot camp sergeants and officers fought in World War II, as well. They survived. Two hundred ninety-three thousand, nine hundred eighty-six Americans were killed. It was the toughest boot camp in the world.

I had a question: Could I measure up to those who were fighting and dying for me when I was a little kid making faces for chocolate, or calling President Truman a son-of-a-bitch? How many of the Marine sergeants and officers around me lost friends on the islands of Guadalcanal and Tarawa, or some anonymous numbered hill, or the Chosin Reservoir in the place called Korea?

Later, I would study battles at Yorktown, Gettysburg, Little Big Horn, Belleau Wood, Iwo Jima, Normandy, Monte Casino, Inchon and Khe Sanh, where Americans had died. I salute them every day, every single day. I wonder, this Memorial Day, how many of those laughing boys in uniform on the train I rode from El Paso to Los Angeles with, twenty three months after Pearl Harbor, died for freedom? How many died for me?

Quien Soy Yo

Maricela M. Aguilar

Growing up in Dallas, Texas, I never had much exposure to Latino culture in the mainstream community. Being Mexican-American meant keeping the family traditions and customs at home, bringing them out only during Anglo-recognized celebrations, such as *Cinco de Mayo* and *Diez y Seis de Septiembre*. At the celebrations, only the really traditional stuff was expected, like the food, which included *tostadas, tacos, tamales* and such, and of course the folklorico dancers, in their beautifully colored outfits.

So, it was to be expected that when I became an adult, I would have a yearning to know more about my Latino background. I knew there was more to me than *tacos, tortillas,* and *"el jarabe tapatio."* I felt the need to read and explore how the Mexican part of me, and the American part of me, came to be, and what that meant.

As I raised my family and got involved in the community, I learned that there were many contributions people like me had made, were making, and would continue to make. I met people like Jose Angel Gutierrez, one of the founders of the *Raza Unida Party*, birthed during the Chicano movement. I met Martha Cotera and Diana Flores, women who had lived the Chicano movement and were determined to continue it in their own manner. I read Chicano literature and met the likes of Rodolfo Anaya, Sandra Cisneros, and Carmen Tafolla – people who, through their writing, opened my eyes to my culture.

Through all of this, I gained a renewed sense of who I was and who I wanted my children to be. Although I didn't realize it, I guess my search for understanding my culture encompassed my whole family. When I decided to participate in a friend's event where I would read Chicano writings aloud, my youngest son approached me with a poem he had written for me. After reading it, I decided my search for cultural identity was over and my quest to share my Chicano heritage had begun!

Quien Soy Yo

For Mom -- Alejandro Trevino

From spilled blood is where I come.
This blood I carry in my veins comes from many
different cultures
And many different peoples.
I carry in me the beauty and strength of an Aztec
Princess,
The knowledge and skills of an Indian mother,
La fuerza de las Adelitas*,
Y el orgullo de ser Tejana.
Bring these all together with their beauties and
strengths and you have me.
Una mujer; beautiful, brown and proud, una Chicana!

* Adelitas, Mexican women soldiers.

Cariño y Familia
Affection and Family

Cariño really does not translate well into English. It is much richer than affection. Cariño is a true sense of love, of awe, and of gratitude towards another that touches the very soul of existence. Cariño has many forms. A look which shows that you count and are safe, a gentle caress that puts a smile on the heart, or words spoken gently that heal the pain and hurt. Cariño is one of the greatest attributes of our heritage.

Where does our sense of cariño come from? Our family. The family in our culture is second in importance only after our faith. The family is us. There is a deep commitment to protect, to love, and to cherish. For most, it is the source of life, love, joy, unity and strength. From the family comes our sense of self, our values, our hopes, and our dreams.

A Single Mother's Dream

Sylvia Fuentes

I am struck with the thought that mainstream society believes that single mothers do not work, nor do they provide a better quality of life for their children. "Nombre, another generation of welfare. Damn Mexicans, all they do is reproduce and dropout of school." All of my life I wanted a college education. I used to tell people that I went to college for two years and dropped out to get married – and I wasn't even pregnant! In other words, I had no business dropping out or getting married. The marriage only lasted seven years, but out of it came my two wonderful children, Elena and Alejandro. This is our story.

There was a time when I questioned myself constantly about getting divorced. Did I do the right thing? How much will my children suffer without two parents? Can I afford it? Will my children understand? Yes, I did the right thing. My children were blessed with a father that "stuck" around when they were little. However, I soon discovered that the laws in the United States almost guaranteed that the woman who has custody of the children would live in poverty.

It was in the mid-eighties when I first realized that somehow I was not going to be a statistic. I remember vividly, I was at a conference in Chicago, Illinois. Juan Andrade Jr. was the keynote speaker. He stated: "By the year 2000, we (Hispanics/Latinos/as) will be the largest minority, the least educated, and our women and children will live below the poverty line!" I remember feeling a sense of desperation. I thought about my two babies. Somehow I knew that I had to go back to school.

"No man is an island." No woman is an island either. For me to have gotten to where I am today, I must acknowledge my *familia*. My beloved father, Antonio Fuentes, passed away in 1978, but taught me about the man who cried because he did not have shoes...until he met the man who did not have feet. My mother, Sara Fuentes, strength and faith is unwavering. My sister Cristina has always been the one person who has never stopped believing in my potential. My sister Diana continues to teach me about financial freedom. Finally, there is Elena and Alejandro. It is ironic that when I asked them if they wanted to submit an essay, they each had one already. It seems that my daughter wrote her essay, which made me cry, for a project entitled: <u>Menudo for the Hungry Soul</u>. Alejandro had written his essay for an English class. Both of their essays were about me and needless to say, I was both honored and humbled by what they had written. In conclusion, I would like to send a message to all parents: I promise you that if you know where your children are at all times, and you know who their friends are, you have won half of the battle. Oh, by the way, Mr. Andrade, Jr. and I received our doctorates on the same day from the same school. I did not know this until they called his name.

Single Mother

Maria Palacios

Single Mother!
Words that splatter like rotten eggs
Against my conscience
Every time my children ask,
"When is Daddy coming back?"

Single Mother!
I pretend to enjoy the baseball game
They used to watch with him
While searching for answers
Still too young to understand.

Single Mother!
Children need their father
Years of a bitter man
And five children
Who never saw him sober.

Single Mother!
I hear them say.
That's why I've learned
To make airplanes out of paper.

Family Tree

Gilda Garza

When Andrea was a senior in high school, her goal was to receive a "Rosette" in the annual art exhibition sponsored by the county. She chose an oil canvas for her project and decided to draw the "Family Tree." She drew the countries which her ancestors were from and gave a little history of each generation.

Andrea's grandparents were role models. Her grandfather earned a living any way that he could; initially chopping wood, milking cows, hoeing and picking cotton, setting and topping onions, hauling hay, shearing sheep, and eventually doing construction work.

Her grandmother was a homemaker. Having eight children she worked just as hard at home as her husband did out in the fields. She fed her children well, washed clothes by hand, and hung clothes outside on the clothesline. She home-starched and ironed, sewed and mended, made one or two quilts per year, made tortillas twice a day, and always had supper on the table for her husband. She even had time for a flower garden.

It was inspiring to reminisce about their obligation to their children. Coming from a low-income family, they did not provide the best for their family; rather they provided the best they could afford. They encouraged family unity, religious practice, and most importantly, family values!

Andrea received her "Rosette" award and "The Best of Show." However, as descendants, we are the grand prize recipients...a grand prize and a legacy of love, faith and values.

A Gift from God

Rita Urias Mendoza

I grew up in a large family with nine kids where everyone worked and shared. I was loved, but in those days there was seldom any hugging and kissing. It is from this background that I have written the following letter to my daughter, who is a gift from God:

Dear Marcella, my first born, my love,

God brought you to me so that I would learn to love in the open. It was through you that I no longer loved in secret. I went public with my show of affection. I can envision myself in the small apartment in Spokane, holding you and being engulfed by the wonderful, great love I felt for you. I thought to myself, *I cannot contain this love – my heart will surely burst.*

We grew up together, you and I. Sometimes apart – sometimes alone – as we each pursued our individual interests. Always there was the knowledge that we had unconditional love for each other, as we still do today.

Knowing the Holy Spirit dwells in you, as He does in me, strengthens the rope that binds us. A "rope that cannot be broken" holds us. I picture our Lady of Guadalupe, nuestra Virgen Morena (*our dark-skinned Virgin*), crocheting an everlasting cord—never ending—as yet another loop extends to those you love. As my thread tends to fray, my Lord sends me a surge of fresh love to hold me together even more firmly than before. Tu, mi Hija, (you, my daughter), are strength and joy. You are truly a gift from God.

Doogle's Buddy

Milena Canal

This story is about love, hope and faith. My father and my son, Christopher, had one of the closest relationships you ever saw between a grandfather and a grandson. My father, an American-Colombian, loved all of his grandchildren and loved spending as much of his retirement time with them as he could. Fortunately, he lived close enough to have dinner with Christopher and I at least a few times a week, as well as spending many Sundays at our home. He was an excellent role model as a metallurgical engineer and designer. Dad always encouraged my son to draw on his drafting board and be creative. Since the moment Christopher could begin recognizing anyone, he would just light up when "Doogle" came into the room. Doogle was my Dad's nickname. As time passed and Christopher began to get around, these two were inseparable, going on walks, raking the yard, with father simply being my little boy's personal jungle gym. Many times I came home when Christopher was literally crawling on Doogle's head.

A couple of months before Christopher's fifth birthday, Doogle called me and said he wasn't feeling well. He was hospitalized with severe heart troubles for twelve days. After the first couple of days of his hospitalization, I came home to my four-year-old, who was diligently trying to write a note. He asked me how to spell "Dear God." After I told him the letters, he began feverishly scribbling a letter. I asked if he wanted me to continue helping him write the words for his letter, and he said, "God understands what I am writing, but thanks anyway." With great detail he folded the note carefully, hole-punched the corner, and took the helium "Get Well" balloon that Doogle let him bring home from the hospital and tied the string around the note. Moments passed. Then I heard the door slam and he came running in whooping and cheering, "Yes!" He had successfully released the balloon and no trees had stopped it from reaching God. He was confident that Doogle would get well after God received his note. This became a daily ritual for Chris.

On Valentine's Day, I arrived with balloons and chocolates in hand to visit my Dad. The hospital was going to release him to my care the next day. Nurses gathered around and said he had been patiently waiting. I gave him a hug and we said a few words. Within fifteen minutes, these words were to be his last moments. Returning home that evening I told Chris we did not need any more balloons for his nightly note sending. He knew instantly. "Doogle's dead!" he screamed. He jumped off the counter, ran to the refrigerator and grabbed tattered photos of himself and friends. He put them in a Valentine's bag and had insisted on getting enough helium balloons to lift these photos to the heavens, so his grandfather would never forget him. He was Doogle's buddy.

In Loving Memory of my father, Jose Roberto Canal.

My Family, My Heroes

Alida S. Hernandez

In a harbor, two ships sailed: one setting forth on a voyage, the other coming home to port. Everyone cheered the ship going out. But the ship sailing in was scarcely noticed. To this, a wise man said: *"Do not rejoice over a ship setting out to sea, for you cannot know what terrible storms it may encounter and what fearful dangers it may have to endure. Rejoice rather over the ship that has safely reached port and brings its passengers home in peace. And this is the way of the world: when a child is born, all rejoice, when someone dies, all weep. We should do the opposite. For no one can tell what trials and travails (to labor hard) await a new-born child, but when a mortal dies in peace, we should rejoice, for he has completed a long journey, and there is no greater boon (blessing) than to leave this world with the imperishable crown of a good name,"* ...The Talmud.

I was deeply moved when I read the lines above. They made me recall my father's question to my sister the day before he died: "Was it worth it?" he asked.

My sister replied: "Of course, it was worth it. You had a wife and seven children who loved you very much." He grabbed her hand and somehow felt a lot better about his life. To have touched so many lives and left a good name was, in fact, quite an accomplishment.

A person often sums up, or takes an inventory of, his or her life in the face of death. For that reason, life should be lived to its fullest. I try to live my life this way and I look to the influences of my family for guidance.

My father, Arnaldo Salinas, left us with so many good memories and lessons. He was the type of person who would never say a harsh word about anyone. He was a self-educated man who could disassemble a car engine and put it back together without a reference manual. He lived a good life. He believed in God, yet never really went to church unless one of his daughters was getting married. He used to say he "talked to God" throughout his day. He loved the outdoors and being close to nature. The animals at the ranch provided a tremendous source of entertainment for him. The way that he dealt with tragedies gave us an example of how to accept the realities of life.

My mother, Eva, at seventy-four, is quite a spirited lady. She has a terrific sense of humor even though she has had to deal with much sadness in her life. She lost her father when she was fifteen and had to work alongside her mother to support the family. She worked in the fields with my father to help make ends meet. When my sister, Adelaida, was afflicted with polio at nine months of age, my mother could not accompany her baby to Louisiana for surgery. There was simply no money. Only a mother could understand the anguish she must have felt.

My mother had to care for our elderly grandmother until her death and later, care for my father during his last illness. It seems as though this was all the pain a person could endure, yet she had to deal with the trauma of seeing my brother incarcerated for three years.

Nevertheless, these wonderful and loving role models have served as our heroes. They taught me and my four sisters and two brothers how to deal with life, regardless of the circumstances. All the women in my family seemed to have learned this lesson and their lives are inspirational to me.

My sister Adelaida, who is now confined to a wheelchair, has earned a college degree and is a self-sufficient woman, despite her tragic car accident and subsequent surgeries.

She is completely independent and is never limited by her disability. We recently went to Nuevo Progreso to celebrate another sister's birthday. The bumpy sidewalks were never an obstacle for her. She kept telling us, "Yes, let's go." Never seeing a problem. She reminds me how small my own perceived barriers really are.

My sister Aida, has been an attorney in McAllen since 1977. She was the first female Assistant District Attorney in Hidalgo County. She helps a great deal of people in her practice, and manages to care for her husband and three children, one of whom has a difficult illness. She makes everything look easy. Aida calls me to a greater understanding of my own abilities.

My sister Alma, is one of the greatest homemakers I know. She is raising three children, while caring for the needs of others as a social worker. She re-instills in me a sense of family and tradition that I lose sight of sometimes.

Then there's Alicia. She has had the responsibility of living at the family ranch along with my mother. She raises cattle, sheep and goats, and sells Frito-Lay products. She has a degree in animal husbandry and we all look forward to the day she becomes a veterinarian. Alicia reminds me of my father's world and the sacredness of nature.

My husband, Marcos, and my two daughters, Laura Liza and Lebeth Lamar, have been behind me one hundred percent. They are a constant reminder of my greatest challenge, which is to set an example that will last a lifetime.

As for myself, I began my career as a farm worker and have since become the co-owner of a successful employment agency. I feel compelled to mention Jennie Morehead, my partner, as part of my family. She has been with me for many years, through good and bad times, always consistent in her love and commitment to our friendship and our business. Her strength and tenacity have lifted me in some of my darkest hours.

Sometimes, people ask me, "Why are you so active?" I guess the reason is because I feel like I have so much to give. I've been lucky. I draw my strength and power from a large, deeply rooted tree that continues to branch out, reaching ever for the sky.

Gift

Teresa Perez

When I was young, before my teenage years, my mother and I would talk from time to time about her life as a little girl. Her father was a shoe cobbler in the 1920's. Since her family was poor, Mom would tell me how they would "make do" any way they could. One time, she told me they used newspaper as toilet tissue! And they would sew their own clothes using newspapers to make patterns. Before I was born, before too many children left her very little spare time, my mother had been a wonderful seamstress, as had her mother.

One summer afternoon, my mom described a typical Christmas when she was growing up. Her voice was animated as she described the food: empanadas, tamales, and dainty cinnamon/sugar cookies that melted in your mouth, etc. Then she started to tell me about the gifts her brothers and sisters received at Christmas. By the tone of her voice and look in her eyes, I imagined the wonderful gifts she must have received – perhaps a new dress, or doll, or some fantastic toy. She described how early one Christmas morning, the children arose to find an old, faded red wagon painted a shiny bright red for her youngest brother. There was an old doll with a freshly washed and mended dress for herself, father's old coat cut down to fit her older brother, and shoes that had been mended and shined for one sister.

Though I did not say anything to my mother that day, or ever as our talks gradually became less frequent, I was shocked by her story! How could she and her brothers and sisters have been happy with those Christmas gifts?

As the years went by, I never forgot this story. And as I matured the story came to mean so much more to me than just children getting short-changed at Christmas. I wonder if children today can feel what I feel when I think back on my mother's Christmas as a child. How her parents struggled to make a Christmas for their children no matter what. How each received gifts that were the creation of their parent's own hands and time. How children were happy and grateful for whatever they received, because back then, Christmas was more of the "spirit" than anything else.

Could children today do without their high-tech toys and name-brand clothes? Could they appreciate something restored and brought back to life, realizing that something "old" is not always to be discarded, but something to be cherished even more so, for all of the wonderful memories? Maybe they would react just like I did when I first heard the story. Can anything that a parent buys mean as much as something that they personally created? Is there anything intrinsic to gifts that are exchanged between families anymore at Christmas-time?

Maybe only time can give one a true appreciation of the real moral of my mom's Christmas story. Did my mother tell me the story to teach me a lesson? Probably not. She was just recalling her childhood. I know now a little more about what made my mother the person she was. She never asked for much. My mother died not ever knowing the impact that her story had on me.

Tribute To My Mother

Maria Palacios

Ay Mamita,
How I wish I had your strength,
the same strength that held you up
when the doctors told you
that your child would never walk.
The same strength that didn't let you fall
when you were left alone
to raise three children,
when you had to wash cloth diapers
in the river
and invent happy thoughts
to make us smile.
How I wish I could laugh
the same way you did when the teachers told you
that your girls needed a father figure;
a symbol of strength.
Little did they know
that you had been a man all your life.
How I wish I could hold back my tears.
With his name written on it.
The way you did
when at dinner we asked for more food
and you split your portion of overcooked rice
between the three of us.
How I wish I had your courage.
The same courage you had
when you came to the States

with nothing but a suitcase full of dreams,
and two words
of mispronounced English on your lips.
I didn't understand it back then
when you said
that a woman didn't need a man to survive.
I see streaks of gray on your head.
Your face looks tired.
Invented happy thoughts
Seem less convincing.
And yet, you continue to be
our pillar of strength,
our fountain of wisdom.
Mami, don't work so hard
we ask.
A familiar gleam appears in your eyes
as you say:
"A woman doesn't need a man to survive."

The Sweetest Flower of All

Evangelina Nino Coy Rangel

My dear Aunt Tomasita was the sweetest, smartest and most beautiful woman I have ever known. She was quiet, well groomed and rich. She never married because she so loved everybody, that she just couldn't give all her love to just one person. Everybody that knew her, admired her. She was the first one in the barrio to have a color TV, the first one to have a telephone, and the first to lend an ear or to dispense good advice. The coffee was always on at her house. I remember my cousin Meme saying that if you were hungry, you could visit Tia Tome and that she would serve you breakfast, lunch and dinner before noon.

Tomasita Nino was a woman who lived way ahead of her time. She was born in 1904, the daughter of a well-to-do Mexican farmer. She was the apple of his eye. He spared no expense where she was concerned, buying her jewels, perfumes, jeweled combs for her beautiful auburn hair, and always telling her how much she was loved. She dared to believe she was special and treated everybody like she was treated. Tia Tome was a self-employed businesswoman. She was a seamstress. She had more business than anyone else I knew. She treated her customers like friends, charging a fair price for her work. And for those that shared her love of gardening, there would be a tour of her beautiful "patio" which she took much pride in.

Her passion was creating beautiful, flowery things. She loved to embroider, crochet and plant flowers. Her backyard was always ablaze with roses, lilies, seasonal flowers, trees that flower, and lots and lots of other flowers. Once Tia gave me a gorgeous card. On the front of it was a picture of an exquisite bouquet of white orchids. When I opened it to read the message, it read, "With our deepest sympathy." It was my fifteenth birthday. Tia couldn't read or write, but she knew how to live and she knew how to love, and Tia Tome was the sweetest and most beautiful flower of all. I miss you Tia.

Tomasita Nino 1904 –1988

Family Values

Alejandro Alaniz

Growing up in my family consisted of two things. The first was that you had to graduate from high school. That is reasonable, I told myself. The second was that you had to graduate from college. I guess this was pretty demanding, but I thought nothing of it. I mean I've been told that I had to go to college for as far back as I can remember. In my house, education was not an option; it was a must. If my sister or I were to say that we didn't want to go to college, my mom's response was always the same: "There is the door." You see my grandfather did not have any formal schooling and my grandmother only made it to the fourth grade. Mom wanted more for us.

I was born in 1979 and grew up in Aurora, Illinois. Other than talking back to my mom, I was a pretty good kid. I avoided gangs and all of that other stuff. I attended a Catholic school that was only a couple of minutes from my house. A single mother who loved us dearly raised my sister, Elena, and me. After school one day I saw my Mom crying. I asked her what was wrong. I got the normal response that parents say when something is wrong: "Nothing. Everything is ok." Later that day, my mom sat my sister and I down at the kitchen table, and with a very sincere face, told us that she had lost her job.

I was only seven years old at the time, and didn't even think anything of it. To a seven-year-old like me, it was more important to see all of my favorite cartoons. The first thing that came to my mind was: "Oh well, I guess she'll have to get another job." It appears that it wasn't that easy, because a couple of weeks later my mom sat us down at the kitchen table again. I thought to myself: "*What now? Did she lose another job?*" It was then that my Mom told us that she wanted to go back to school. My sister and I looked at each other with a puzzled look. We didn't think that Mom going back to school was such a bad idea. My sister and I grew up together and were very close. We were not only brother and sister, we were best friends. So that night we talked and just couldn't understand why our mom was making such a big deal about going back to school. And then it happened. Our mom dropped the bomb on us.

The next thing you know, my sister and I are packing all of our little toys into cardboard boxes. My mom said that we were going to move to some place called DeKalb. My sister and I looked at each other once again, and thought: "*What is DeKalb?*" I could not think straight. I mean, what about all of my friends? What about my family? I just could not comprehend why my mom wanted to go back to school at the age of thirty-five. It was then that my mom told me something that I will never forget for as long as I live. She told me to remember that there will always be someone that can take your job from you, but there is not one person that can take an education from you.

Fast forward to the present. My mom and I enjoy long talks. One day I asked her besides losing her job, what made her go back to school? She said that she valued education so much because her parents worked very hard for her to have a better life.

My "Mama Sara" had to stop going to school because her mom had to work and someone had to take care of the family. My grandpa never went to school because they were so poor that he had to work at the age of seven. My grandpa used to take my mom and her sisters to the fields to pick tomatoes, so that they could see what they had to look forward to if they did not go to school. My mom did something similar to me. She made me get a summer job. It was the worst summer of my life, working at a book factory.

I was working ten-hour shifts, seven days a week. I lifted boxes full of books for ten hours straight. Sure it was good money, but I don't know if it was worth it. I mean, I would come home and go straight to bed. After that summer, I was sure of two things. I knew that whatever I did, I was not going to drop out of college. And I was sure that I wanted to finish college and go to law school.

Currently, I am a junior in college and my sister graduated in December of 1999. Oh yeah, Mom finished college and received her doctorate. It has been a long hard road for all of us, but well worth it. I can't help but wonder if we did not come to this place called DeKalb, where would we be now? I guess we would be lost and without an education. I'm proud of what my mom has accomplished, not only in school, but also at home. Thanks to my mom, my sister and I now know the value of an education.

Oh What A Soul!

Lupe A. Davila

It is almost certain that all of us have met someone in our lifetime that was always cutting up, happy, cracking jokes, making others laugh, and acting mischievous in any possible way. The nickname I had for that someone I knew was "travieso." I can still hear his sneaky laugh whenever he got caught doing something he should not be doing. His laughter was like the laughter of a little kid caught doing something wrong, and enjoying the delicious moment of doing it and getting caught. This "travieso" was my father.

The fact that he had a child who was born when he was in his fifties, only contributed to his machismo. He acted like an old rooster, crowing his delight at having a young child. Mexican chauvinism being what it is in Mexican men, he was proud of having a young daughter. Mom was not thrilled at having a young kid around when she was middle-aged and tired. After all, I am the youngest of nine children.

When I was a very young child we moved from the barrio to a predominately Anglo neighborhood. My mom was in poor health and Dad took over a lot of the duties like packing my lunch, talking to me about becoming a lady, working with me on my schoolwork, and making sure I understood right from wrong. We would sit and visit about the past and the future. He would tell me stories about the turn of the century and how his family had fled to the local church when 1900 had arrived, in fear that the world was coming to an end. He shared the horrors of immigrating into the United States and how hard it was to get started in a country where you could not speak the language. The profession he chose to enter was "la cocina." He first went to work as a chef's personal assistant, learned the ropes, and soon became the primary chef at one of the largest hotels in our hometown.

Dad was semi-retired by the time I entered high school. He would drive me to school and I would take the bus home. I would find him waiting for me on our front porch when I returned. He was always ready to visit. He had taken a job cooking for a company only during the lunch hour, so he was home by the time I got home.

Education was a big deal for him. To my dad, high school graduation had the equivalent meaning of a master's degree. He encouraged me to work in white-collar atmospheres and discouraged me from jobs that did not pay well.

When I opted to marry young, he was very disappointed, even though he loved my choice of a husband. Dad was very concerned when I had my first child and then had my second child only a year later. In as kind a manner as he could, he asked if my plans were to have a child a year.

Dad and Mom were married in excess of fifty years when she died. My concern for him when she died prompted me to encourage him to go the local senior citizen's center. Little did I know what this would mean for my father and his life. He rediscovered sex and acted like a goofy teenager with his hormones on the loose. It was really something to see an eighty-year-old man being chased by elderly ladies. Since he was still driving his car, he was very popular and quite a party guy. He loved to sing with mariachis, although you would often find him singing, regardless of the music. If it was fun, he was there. His mission, he said, was to spread good cheer and to be of service to other people – particularly the ladies – whenever he could.

Cancer first paid him a visit over twenty years ago. We were getting ready to go on vacation. My husband and I had gone to Dad's house to pick him up to take him with us when I noticed a lump on his shoulder. Within hours, we were in the hospital and the doctors were saying it was bad. The tumor was malignant and the prognosis was not good.

Dad was victorious in that battle. He refused medication and went on with his life. His positive attitude, his belief in God, and his tenacity and penchant for life kept him going. In the meantime, I became a grandmother. Through my brothers and sisters, he became a great, great grandfather. He was the head of a family with five generations. He traveled to the East Coast with my husband and me, to marry off our daughter. He traveled to visit us every three months or so when we lived in Memphis, Tennessee, and then to our current home in Houston, Texas. Dad had never been on a plane until my husband got transferred and we moved. He became a real jet-setter then.

The memories are so many. The most vivid are the ones of the last year of his life as he battled prostate cancer. I have a videotape of Dad singing in October of the year he died where you see a sick man, but a happy man, standing with a cane, raising his voice in song, singing his heart out, only to die in December.

Though he is gone, he really is not. He will always live in us. His memory is fresh. Whenever I have a dilemma or feel as though I need someone to speak to, I hold still and think of my dad. That wonderful chef who is probably cooking up a storm in heaven; he did his job well. He is my "travieso," my wonderful, beautiful dad.

Fe y Esperanza

Faith and Hope

Faith is at the core of our existence. We believe in God, the Mother Mary, Jesus and all the Saints. There is a deep sense of connection with spirit and we believe that *primero Dios*. That means, you put God first and the rest will be okay. Our faith restores our tired spirits and gives us comfort. It also renews and energizes us. It is our source.

Hope is one of the greatest gifts of our faith. Even in the darkest hour, we feel in our heart of hearts that God is with us, protecting us. He is urging us on past our fears to continue on our path with optimism of a brighter tomorrow.

God Hears Us

Ellen Castro

I want to share with you an experience that to this day
fills me with wonderment, love and faith.

It was November 6, 1996. I had chosen to return to
Boston to heal and release the painful memories associated
with my graduate degree from Harvard at the age of thirty-
six. The years 1987-1988 had been the most difficult year
of my life. I was struggling to regain my self-esteem after a
failed marriage to an abusive husband, and the end of a
promising career at Exxon Co. USA due to depression
brought on by discrimination, sexual harassment and a
tragic childhood.

I felt so desperately lonely. Alone in Cambridge, I was
contemplating suicide when by grace, a dear friend came to
visit and took me to the health center. I once again entered
counseling to get to the core of my desperation.
Desperation had led me to be gamut of unhealthy
behaviors...overeating, over-drinking, and looking for
comfort in the arms of unhealthy men.

Now fast forward to 1996. My life was so much better. I
had curbed my appetite for drama and self-destruction. I
was healthier and owned my own business, a beautiful
home, and was caretaker of an incredible cat named Pepito,
or Mr. P. (another miracle). I was beginning to truly love my
resilience and myself.

I spent November 5th visiting the Harvard campus and
my old hangouts, crying and letting go of the emotions and
pain. I awoke November 6th knowing it was time to catch a

flight to Dallas. I was done. It was time to go home. Of course, I had to walk first to Faneuil Hall and eat delicious clam chowder. On the way back to the hotel, I decided to stop at a church across the street. I so wanted to thank God for the miracle of my life and the wonders that had occurred in the last eight years.

I kneeled and sobbed, releasing all my anguish, pain and sadness. I sobbed even more when I thought how far I had come...for God's grace. I prayed and besieged God to please help me continue on my path of love, light and peace. I looked up and there was this incredible stained glass window of Jesus Christ with outstretched arms.

I sobbed louder as I felt an overwhelming sense of peace, comfort and safety flow through my body. Once again, I prayed to God that I would remember such a moment of unconditional love. I left the church, returned to my room and checked out.

I remember the effortless cab ride to Logan Airport. I was crying silently with gratitude. Let me briefly describe Logan Airport. It is huge with miles and miles of curbs. The cabbie stopped. I paid and jumped out. Next to my little toe was something shiny. Not having my glasses on, I merely put it in my pocket. I proceeded to the counter where the agent smiled and told me there would be no charge for changing my ticket...yet another miracle?

I went to sit down and await my flight. I took out the shiny object. As I gazed upon it, I began to cry. I had found a tin medallion, which duplicated the stained glass window of Jesus with his outstretched arms. God had heard and acted on my prayers.

To this day, when I need a physical reminder of God's miraculous love and healing touch, I look in my jewelry box. The tin image of Jesus twinkles at me, beckons me to wear it, and once again, my faith is restored.

A Glimpse of Light

Roxanne Del Rio

What does God have in store for us during our short time here on earth? Each second, minute, hour, day, week, month, and year passes so quickly. We're free to spend these fleeting moments as we wish, but if we're smart, we'll live each day to the fullest. Because the old saying is true: "We never know when we'll be here today and gone tomorrow."

Early one summer evening last year, I experienced a near-fatal car accident. I was driving to my aerobics class when it happened. As I approached the intersection, I stopped to look for traffic. But when I crossed the street, a truck appeared out of nowhere and crashed into the driver's side of my car. The sixteen-year-old behind the wheel was drag racing another teenager at seventy-five miles per hour on a residential street with a speed limit of twenty miles per hour. I don't remember much about the accident, but eyewitnesses say that my car became airborne, landed on the ground, and spun around until it hit a street sign.

The emergency crew arrived within minutes and found me unconscious. I don't remember any of this, but I do remember a strong, authoritarian, but loving, voice says to me, "Roxanne, you've been in an accident. Everything is going to be OK." I didn't panic and I didn't feel any pain. Somehow, I knew I was in good hands.

Shortly after that, I felt myself drift upward with someone toward an unidentifiable place. My companion and I walked down an unfamiliar hallway. On the right side of the hall, I saw a very dark and strange entrance. The darkness scared me, so I looked to my left, where a glimpse of light caught my attention. It was as though the light were calling me. I instinctively knew I must follow the path to the left. As I followed the light, it got brighter. I remember feeling overcome with happiness.

When I was just inches away from the light, I saw people dressed in white robes with gold belts tied around their waists standing in line. But I didn't have a white robe; I was still in my aerobics outfit. I didn't recognize any of these people. Although everyone seemed very happy, no one was talking. It was very quiet.

I stood there and just watched the beaming white light and the people who were walking into it. My mind was filled with questions. What's going on? Who are these people and how are they passing through the light? I remember realizing how peaceful and happy I felt standing before the light. I truly felt loved, safe, and without a worry in the world. No words can express the beauty of the beaming light. The soft white clouds looked incredible, full of shadows and reflections, and illuminated by this brilliant light, which was white, yellow and gold.

As I stood there watching, I again realized that I was not alone. Someone was standing to the left of me. I believe it was my guardian angel. I never saw his face, but I knew he was the same person who had escorted me to this wonderful place. He knew my name, and I felt as if he and I had been friends all my life.

I also wanted to walk through the light, so I got in line. When it was my turn, I lifted my right leg to leap through, but I felt a strong force. It was my guardian angel. He had stopped me. I remember his exact words: "Roxanne, it's not your time yet." And at that moment, I opened my eyes. I was in a hospital bed in the emergency room of Parkland Hospital in Dallas. The doctors and nurses began to explain what had happened, but all I could focus on was the beautiful, loving light that I had experienced. Not much else mattered. I was calm, and still had the same feeling of happiness and serenity that I had standing before the light. I felt as if I had just awakened from a long restful sleep. I had never experienced a better sleep than that.

Eventually, I began to feel the aches and pains in my body. That evening, I had undergone a series of tests and x-rays. The doctors stitched up the cut over my left eye, set my broken wrist, removed the tiny pieces of shattered glass from my wounds, and treated my concussion, whiplash and contusions. Two of my dearest friends stood by me in the emergency room. Thank God for friends. Somehow, I knew that I was going to be just fine.

I was released from the hospital that night. It was a miracle that I survived. The doctors and nurses were amazed that I was able to survive the accident, and the eyewitnesses couldn't believe I wasn't crushed. I am convinced that my guardian angel stood between the impact of the other car and me.

I was alive and that was the main thing. The cuts and bruises would eventually go away. Now I had to process what I had experienced. The recovery wasn't easy. At first I couldn't do very much. I regretted the fact that I was once very active and now was forced to do almost nothing. I got angry.

When I returned to work, I called Fr. Felix, a graduate student at the university where I work. Fr. Felix talked to me about my experience with the light. He wanted to know what this glimpse of heaven looked and felt liked. I told him it was like earth, but without the worries or pain or suffering. Everything that I saw, I recognized from my experiences here on earth. Fr. Felix and I found the lesson: That earth can be heaven. We must live each day according to God's will. If we listen to Him during prayer, He will guide us to do His will. We don't have to wait to get to heaven to be happy. We can be happy here on earth, if we learn to surrender all our pains and sorrows to Him, and trust that He will take care of us. I realized that this accident was perhaps meant to be. It was God's way of giving me a glimpse of what He has in store for us as we journey to our next life. My anger lifted and I began the process of healing emotionally.

In January of that same year, I began spending one hour a week in adoration, before the Blessed Sacrament in addition to attending daily mass. One day during Adoration, I began to wonder how I would react if the icons of Jesus or Mary began to weep. You hear stories about miracles taking place when and where you least expect. I should be so lucky! But what if I witnessed something this phenomenal? Who would believe me? It really doesn't matter. I firmly believe that God gave me a wonderful glimpse of what He has waiting for us.

Fr. Felix encouraged me to write about this near-death experience. I want to encourage you to live each day to the fullest. You don't have to wait until you are dead to experience heaven, because heaven can be experienced on earth. Life here on earth is preparing us for another life to come in heaven. But first we must realize the importance of life here on earth. Also, when God calls you to join Him, you won't be afraid, for the love that is waiting for you is awesome.

For those of you who wonder what happened to the sixteen-year-old, he walked away with a broken finger. But I have learned to forgive and forget. I know that each unfortunate experience has its positive side. It has been a year since the accident, and the only time I am reminded of the accident is when the weather changes and my wrist twinges a little. As for the people in white robes, I believe they were souls waiting to go through the gates of heaven. And I firmly believe that God, in His goodness, has given each of us our own guardian angel to guard and protect us.

Thank you God, for Guardian Angels!

Alexis

Eloise Castro

I believe that all of us need a special place. It should be a place where we can go to find peace, quiet time, to meditate, or to reflect our yesterdays, our present, and our hopes for the future. It is a place to go when we have no other place to hide or escape.

For me this special place is called The Grotto. I have been going to The Grotto for many years. I usually go there when I have no other place to go. There, I have found many answers to my pleas and have been shown many miracles. One special miracle, or sign from God, always remains with me.

Several years ago, I was very depressed. My apartment was very small. All I could do was stay in bed or go to my closet and hide there. I look back now and I'm not sure what I was hiding from, but most likely it was my fears. I can still remember the feelings of deep despair and uselessness, of feeling alone, of turmoil, and fear. I asked myself over and over again why I should go on. I remember feeling like this for days. I just did not care. I felt paralyzed. I found that I didn't care how I looked or even if I was clean.

I was alone, expect for my little teacup poodle named Alexis. I believe now that Alexis was one of God's little gifts. I remember being in bed with my blanket up to my nose. I was praying to God to give me a sign that it would be all right. *Please give me some peace or please let me die.* I kept repeating this same prayer over and over. Then suddenly, Alexis jumped up on the bed and started to lick me. I knew I needed to get up and feed her and also, I remembered the appointment I had made for her to be groomed. I did not want to do either; I did not have the energy. It took everything I had to get out of bed and take Alexis to the groomer. Now, I would have some time to decide how I could end my life.

Driving back to my apartment, my car seemed to be guided by some force other than myself and I found myself parked at The Grotto. I got out of my car and started to walk. Of all the times I had been to The Grotto, I couldn't recall seeing doves before. I had seen squirrels and many different birds, but never white doves. The doves just stood there despite the fact that Mass had just ended and many people were walking by. Strangely, no one seemed to notice the doves. It seemed that I was the only one seeing these beautiful birds. As I looked around, I saw an ex-nun named Nancy. I went to her and asked her, "Do you see what I see?"

She said, "Yes, there are two white doves." I had such a smile on my face and began to tell Nancy my prayers.

She said, "Eloise, God has answered your prayer." She asked me, "Do you know what the white doves mean?"

I said, "Yes, they are a symbol of peace and the Holy Spirit."

Nancy said, "Eloise, in all the years that I have worked at The Grotto, I have never seen white doves."

I believe God answered my prayers through Alexis. And though she is now only with me in my heart, I know she was my special gift from God.

Mi Abuelita

Maria R. Velasco

That morning I had nowhere to be. I had all day to do whatever I wanted. I stopped to think for a moment. Then everything in the room slowed down until it stopped. I noticed the sun was not shining through the window and the birds had stopped singing their morning song. Everything was still. Time closed in on me like a blue cloud creeping, covering me with a blanket of sadness. I felt it surface from inside, from a still tiny place in my heart. I recognized the feeling realizing that nothing could take it away. I would have to accept it.

I will never ever forget her. I think of her every day. But today, this familiar sadness reminded me of how much a part of me she is. And how much, how so very much, I miss mi Abuelita. I began to drown in my loneliness for her. "Ama, Ama," I cried to the sky weeping like her lost and lonely child of forty-three. My body became weak. The pain rolled in, around and through my heart, reminding me of how much, how so very much, I love her. I've never loved anyone as much as I loved her. And I will for all of my life. My wish to see her was so strong that I wanted to die for a moment just so I could see my Abuelita's face again. I know she is alive, alive in my sadness. She is alive in my longing for her embrace.

In my mind, I asked God, and myself, "Is this going to be another one of those lonely days? No mother, no lover, no child? Will this never end? How much more must I take?" I put on my dark glasses and let my hair hang in hopes of masking my face, which did not feel normal. My voice became weak. My words spilled like tears from my mouth.

Then I remembered I had promised to do Mauri a favor. Mauricio, el joven, talked and made me laugh as I drove him to his English class. The place was right next to St. Edwards. It's that little church where on Easter Sunday, the Aztecas followed the procession drumming and dancing under the eye of the blue moon. I remember looking up at the turquoise sky, my heart beating like the drum. I could feel infinity in my soul.

Waking up from my daydream, I stopped the car and turned to Mauri. "Gracias por alivianarme," le dije. He did not want to see me sad.

He did not want to be reminded of his own sadness. "Dios te bendiga y aprende Ingles, muchacho. Asi, I can speak English with you." He thanked me with caring eyes and a warm smile.

I was treating him with kindness the way Abuelita taught me. She's the one who planted love, the bread of life, into my soul. I felt a little better and I wondered what my day would be like.

I drove a couple of blocks away and lo and behold, I saw...Abuelita? Standing on a corner leaning on her walking cane firmly in front of her. The handicap bus had broken down in the middle of the street and she, the lone rider, had to get off. I passed by with my eyes on her and then made a u-turn, stopping in front of her and the driver.

I recognized her Abuelita skirt, long to her ankles. I recognized the dignity with which she held her head. I got out of the car and approached them. The driver was standing there beside her with his arms in the air holding a piece of paper in his hand. I said, "Can I help? I can take her where she needs to go, if I may."

"Here's where she's going," he said, showing me the name and address.

"Oh yes, I just came from there."

"Muchas gracias," me dijo. Hablando en Espanol con la señora dije.

"Please, Señora, wait a moment while I prepare the seat for you. May I take your arm? Be careful...watch your step...take your time," I said gently.

"Yo se," she said emphatically.

"May I help you with your seat belt?"

"Si," she said.

Someone's Abuelita looked like royalty. In an instant she became my queen. She had gold and silver rings on all of her fingers, and shiny pins on her soft white sweater and knit cap. Everything was pretty and shiny against her dark wrinkly skin. Even her thick glasses shined like diamonds. Her neck was draped with necklaces, pearl and golden. "How beautiful you look, Señora." I sighed, smiling upon her. "Where are you from?"

"Soy Mejicana de Tejas." She lives thirty miles away. "Vengo aqui todos los dias," she said as she reached for me to help her out of the car. We walked slowly down the steps, arm in arm. She led as I walked her to join the others. Everyone was arriving at the same time. She let go as the señora motioned for her to join them. "Gracias," she said.

I bowed to kiss her hand and began walking away. I turned, still dazed by her presence as my eyes searched for one last glimpse of her. But she had disappeared into the crowd. She was gone, yet somehow I knew she was there. And, she was watching me like a guardian angel. I know she was sent to me. It was as if I had died and gone to heaven. The birds began to sing their sunrise song as my heart arose freeing the sadness. I remember watching her as she walked away...taking my pain and leaving only a memory of love.

A Story of Hope and Fried Chicken

Betty Swinners

I really like fried chicken, always have. I think the first time I ate fried chicken I was about nine years old and looking for food in a dumpster. My brother Jerry was with me and I was trying to find food to feed us. My brother was about nine years older and he was mentally disabled. I always knew him as my brother, even though he was not my mother's biological son. You see, my mother was a "curandera" and a lady gave my mother this boy as payment for a "trabajo" she had done. That was before I was even born. I took care of him and he took care of me. I remember being little and him holding my hand as we crossed the streets together. The homeless people and those who others would identify as "wino's," were so nice to us. They gave us candy and donuts from the donut shop's dumpster.

It wasn't always like this. Before, we would run to "Honey Bee's" House, an old black lady who walked with a cane, and she would say, "Hi babies! Ya'll must be hungry. Here is some cornbread and beans." Man, that stuff was good. It didn't matter how drunk Honey Bee was, she would always fix us food. But then, Honey Bee died. We went to her house and her evil twin sister was there. She ran us off with a broom. But the donuts were good, especially the jelly ones. Sometimes they had cigarette ashes on them, but we would wipe it off. I can almost taste the ashes on the donuts now.

I don't have many memories of the past. Maybe I have only selected memory to eliminate the pain. I don't remember my mother ever being kind or saying a kind word.

I don't even remember when we first started living on the streets or how it happened. It seemed that one day I was a little girl in a house that was small, and then next I was a little girl trying to find a home for us to live at.

I did find a home. My brother and I were searching in the dumpster for books. I was trying to learn how to read. Right next to where this building was sat a little vacant house. I went inside. It had no windows, toilet or tub, and there were holes in the floor, but I guessed it would do. Better yet, there was a chicken place right across the street and a donut shop was right around the corner.

I started looking in all the dumpsters for stuff to fix the house. I made a bed on the floor with cardboard, and covered the windows with old screens and plywood. There was no light, water or gas. Not that I knew what that really was. My mother always had candles so I assumed that's the way the house was lit. It got tough when it was cold. I had to do something to keep my mother and brother warm, so I went to the junkyard nearby and rolled an empty barrel home. I filled it with wood and started a fire. What a blessing; it was so warm. It was great to cook food or heat up chicken. We didn't have water, so my brother would bring buckets of water from the building next door for us to bathe in. We used a bucket for the other stuff, because there was no toilet.

One day near Christmas, a businesswoman came by our home and told my mother that I need to go to school or I would be taken away. School? I had to dig around for food during the day!

I got enrolled in school. I was ten by now, so I was put in second grade. After that year, I did not go back to school again, until another lady came and said I was twelve and needed to be in school or else. So here I went again, but now to fifth grade. I had a wonderful teacher. Some kids thought she was the meanest, but she influenced me so much. The school was next to our house. I would jump the fence during lunch and bring my mother and brother my food. Since the cafeteria people knew, sometimes they would add a little extra.

After I finished the fifth grade, I did not go back to school. I worked hard after that and gathered enough money to rent a house for my family. Eventually I went and got a TV, sofa, bed, and other stuff from the resale store. When I was seventeen, I saw a sign that said: "If you have not graduated from high school, get your GED!" Hey, that was me! I barely went to school. Maybe I could go back to school now. Eventually I did attend school during the day and worked at night.

I thank God for "raising" one, for guiding me in the choices I made for my family, and making me the person I am today. As an adult woman I have been called a role model and a leader. It gives me courage to share my story. Sometimes I wonder if I had shared my story before I became a "role model/leader," if I would have even been given the chance to do this. Sometimes I look around me and ask, *what am I doing here and will it ever end*? My message to others is that it does not matter where you come from. What matters is where you are going.

Queta's Story...the first twenty-one years

Enriquetta Garrett

It began on a warm October day in La Habana. Another Cuban girl was born to a middle-class family. Little did she know that the next thirteen years would completely shape her into what she is today.

My early childhood was very happy with a very strong nuclear and extended family. I also had a supportive circle of friends, which have been true "lifelong friends." From very early childhood, I was instilled with very strong values about family, with respect for other's beliefs and ideas, and on education and its benefits and rewards.

However, at the same time, the political situation was starting to heat up in Cuba and even though things were deteriorating around us, our parents always tried to insulate us.

The Cuban Revolution, led by Fidel Castro, was triumphant and came into power on January 1, 1959. At the beginning, everything seemed well and almost everyone was caught up in the euphoria of the moment with high hopes and dreams for the future. Within a few months, though, the atmosphere began to change. I remember my father, who immigrated to Cuba from Spain at the onset of the Spanish Civil War, saying that Castro looked like a communist and that we would probably all have to leave the country. At that time, nobody in the family believed that his statements would become true. Unfortunately, the political and social situations in Cuba started to deteriorate at a quick pace, and my father's predictions came true within two years.

While Cuban teenagers have traditionally been politically active, the Cuban situation accelerated the development of my own consciousness. When I was eleven years old, I had already witnessed the injustices and the systematic unrest that was developing within the students of the country. I had been attending a private Catholic school at the time the government started attacking the churches and all the related institutions. Even though the government did not come into our school and physically harm any of the nuns or the personnel, it forced the school to have government representatives and teachers to monitor what the students would be taught This triggered a lot of unrest. During my first year of secondary school, I became rebellious and would not accept the government propaganda. I would refuse to cooperate with any projects or field trips that I perceived to be supporting the government in any form or fashion. At the end of the year, I joined the national student boycott, refusing to sit for the required official final examination, which resulted in a year of education being nullified.

The continual loss of our individual freedoms, like not being able to freely associate or bring anything purchased into your own home without being scrutinized and constantly watched by the "block committee for the defense of the Revolution" started to take a toll. The unrest in the country continued, and everyday marked an increase of the attacks against governmental and civilian installations. We would hear bombs blasting and routinely witnessed blazes. Even though my family was not involved with any of the counterrevolutionary groups, it was all around us. All this unrest led to an almost total suppression of all individual freedoms. Unbeknown to us, until later, our family's last name was one of those who had been labeled as one that was dangerous to the Revolution.

In the few hours before the "Bay of Pigs Invasion," there were rumors around the city's population that the city of

Havana would be bombarded. Even though we lived in the outskirts of the city, my father decided to temporarily move us to my uncle's house, which had underground living quarters. The whole family basically went into hiding for three days and during that time, up to 100,000 people were apprehended in Havana and held at stadiums, public buildings, and schools, since there were not enough cells to put them in. The reason for this massive arrest of citizens was that they were considered possible supporters of the invading forces that had landed at the Bay of Pigs on the southern coast of the island. We were lucky because the government's militia never located my father. Once this invasion failed and the paranoia settled, my parents were determined to leave the country. My father was able to get all our paperwork to the Venezuelan embassy two days before it closed and we were able to obtain visas/permits to visit our uncle who resided there.

At that time, you were allowed to take only clothing out of Cuba, not money, jewelry or any other articles. On the day of our departure we were singled out as a family, and we were questioned and searched individually by the secret police before we were allowed to board the ship that was to take us to Caracas, Venezuela. We thought that every person that left the country had to go through the same interrogation and search process, and it was not until we boarded the ship that we found out we had been singled out. Thank God they had not found the money my mother was smuggling.

My parents believed that leaving our grandparents and all our possessions would be a temporary situation, and that the whole family would be reunited in a few months. I had just turned thirteen years old before our departure on that November night. As the boat was getting farther from shore and the lights of the city disappeared into the darkness, an overwhelming sadness came over me and I somehow knew that we would never be back.

We arrived in Caracas ten days later. Our nine-month stay in Venezuela was a very rewarding one, since we all learned to appreciate our own individual worth. My brother, my cousin and I won academic scholarships to two of the best Catholic private schools in Caracas, which we gladly took advantage of, even though it meant we had to repeat a grade. The political situation in Venezuela was very unstable at that time and coupled with the fact that my father did not see much improvement for working opportunities in the near future, he came to the realization that we may have to move again. He gathered the family together and informed us that there was the option of going to Spain or we could take our chances in the United States where our former, Cuban next-door neighbor was now residing.

We chose the United States. From the moment we got to the U.S., we strived continually to reunite the rest of the family. Four years later we were able to bring my grandparents and my cousin's parents and sister to reside with us in Dallas, Texas.

We decided to come to the U.S. not knowing any English, except for my brother. He had gone to a private school in Cuba, which was directed by an order of Canadian priests, where they taught half of the curriculum in English. My brother was our voice and navigator in the early 60's when Hispanics were not as visible or prominent in Dallas. Even though we did not have the language skills, we were taken at our word and given proficiency tests in math, science, etc. This allowed us to be placed in high school. My brother and cousin were put in the twelfth grade and I in the tenth.

That first year was very painful because unlike my brother, I did not have my English language skills and I was not allowed to associate with my brother, cousin or any other Hispanic student, nor allowed to speak Spanish at school whether in or out of the classroom. It was a very frustrating time for me, but I never made less than a "C" that first year. Stubbornness and determination carried me through. Even though I was never encouraged to go to college by the high school teachers, counselors or administrators, I was determined that I was going to do it. It had been ingrained in me from an early age, by my family, that, "You can lose everything – but you will always have an education." When my time came to go to college, my father informed me that he could now afford it, but I decided to work for one year before entering the University of Texas at Arlington. I continued to work during my college years and paid for my own education, graduating with a Bachelor of Business and Accounting degree.

"The learning process is ongoing, it never ends."

Believe

Ellen Castro

Believe in yourself
In your divine nature.

Believe that you deserve love and respect
Because you do.

Believe that you make a difference
Make it a positive difference.

Believe that you are worthy of all the beauty and
Abundance of the universe
Because you are!

Believe that all is perfect ... time, place, you
Believe that all is happening for your greatest good
Believe that you are truly loved.

Believe that you can make choices from the heart
Believe that miracles happen
Believe they do.
Believe.

Thank God for Perseverance!

Roxanne Del Rio

I grew up in a family of seven. Mom was a housewife and Dad was a store manager for one of the largest grocery chains in South Texas. I have four siblings and am the middle child.

Growing up was very difficult. I have two sisters and one brother born with birth defects. Every year, some member of my family was in the hospital. My older sister and I were the only ones in the family without health problems. Money was scarce and I remember Christmas without presents.

My sister and I were taught responsibility at an early age. We were caretakers for the house and our brother and two sisters. Mom suffered from major depression and Dad was a workaholic. Although my parents did what they could for my brother and sisters, they had little time for me. So, I thank God for my grandmother. She showed me that she really loved me and she cared for each one of us.

During my senior year in high school, all my classmates were preparing for the prom, graduation and college. Each senior was given an "interest inventory" to determine their possible career paths. The high school counselor also used this inventory to determine success. When I was called into the counselor's office, I was very excited. I was embarking on an adventure. I wanted to go to college. Dad had encouraged all of us to go to college. I remember him saying, "Anyone can take away your material things, but no one can take away your education."

I did not know what career I should select, so I put my fate in the hands of the counselor. "Roxanne, I evaluated your test and it shows that you might want to consider a career in filing, perhaps in the backroom of an office. The test shows that you do not have any communications skills; you cannot communicate with others, much less with the public. And don't bother going to college because you will never be able to obtain a degree." This session knocked what little self-esteem I had right out the window. I struggled in high school and worked hard to get passing grades.

During my senior year, Mrs. Shaw, my literature teacher, told the class to write a descriptive essay about nature. I received a "D" on this paper, but I thought I deserved a "B." She said it was not descriptive enough. Mrs. Shaw told me to "smell the blue and feel the green." But I had no idea what she meant. What does blue smell like and what does green feel like? I began to doubt myself. Could I really have a career, and what should I do for the rest of my life? Was the counselor's assessment of my academic abilities and social skills correct?

Through perseverance, I was determined to attend college. Despite the counselor's advice and my financial obstacles, I registered at a local community college. I applied for financial aid and was blessed with a work-study job on campus. It was during these two years that I began to grow academically. I was placed in remedial classes and accepted the fact I knew, that I had weak academic skills. However, I was blessed with wonderful professors who had confidence that I could succeed. I graduated in two years with an Associate of Arts degree and enrolled as a full-time student at Corpus Christi State University, where I made the "Dean's List."

After graduation, I began working at a community college and decided that I wanted to go to graduate school. I applied and was accepted. However, after two short semesters I had to come home. Mom, Dad and my brother were all in hospital at the same time.

Eventually, I met the man who became my husband. My husband and I moved to Irving, Texas, where I was blessed to find a job at a local university. I decided to continue my graduate education but shortly after I began, my grandmother died. This was very traumatic. Grandma had always been so important to me. I loved her with my whole heart and she had always been there when I needed her. What was I going to do without her? Life was a struggle with working, going to school, and with what would soon be a failed marriage. I graduated with a Master of Public Administration degree from the University of North Texas. The next year, my husband and I divorced after four years of marriage. He had decided that he was in love with someone else.

Shortly after my divorce and the death of my grandmother, I fell into a very deep depression. I felt that I could not survive, despite all the tools and skills I had acquired throughout the years. For the very first time in my life, I felt very alone. I became suicidal. I was overcome by the emotional pain and stress. I called my friends Ana and Rebecca. Ana convinced me not to end my life.

One year later, Mom was diagnosed with pancreatic cancer. She underwent chemotherapy, radiation treatments, and surgery at M.D. Anderson in Houston. For the next eight months, I would drive from Irving to Houston to see her. Although it was difficult, I was glad to have the opportunity to spend quality time with her. Ten months later, Mom died peacefully in our home with all of her family around her.

Each day, I pray for perseverance and the ability to know and do the will of Our Father. Recently I experienced a near-fatal car accident. I was granted the special privilege and grace to experience "the light" that we've all heard about. I can only explain this light as all-consuming and loving. It is a feeling of warmth and the love that Our Father has waiting for us. Life, with its many obstacles and tragedies, can be difficult to endure. But know that you can overcome life's challenges and emotional stresses.

For those of you who like a happy ending, I am recuperating quite well from my accident. I thank God for the wonderful friends who were there for me. Today, I am Director of Admissions for the University of Dallas Graduate School of Management. The graduate school has 2,000 students in its MBA program. I often travel to Latin America and throughout the United States to recruit graduate students and professors, and to establish exchange programs. I conduct many educational workshops and give a number of presentations each year. Who says I can't communicate with the public? The impossible doesn't seem so impossible anymore. I am happy to report that I am now enrolled in a Ph.D. program. Thank you God, for perseverance!

Aspirations

Elena Alaniz

am walking through the park where I am originally from. I see babies having babies. Does this disqualify them from being good parents? I see young Latina women left alone with a baby. I sit on the swing and daydream about my life as a child from a single-parent home. People are shocked. I am not pregnant and I don't have a boyfriend.

I close my eyes and reflect on my life. I am in my last year in college. I am satisfied where I am at this point. Of course, there is always room for improvement.

I do not feel I have missed out on anything being raised in a single-parent home. It is all up to the person and whom they decide to be inspired by. I could have chosen to be like my cousin, who joined a gang. Fortunately, I chose to be like my mother. She has qualities such as: patience, intelligence, strong faith and strong will.

My mother is a very intelligent woman. She has been a single parent for eighteen years. Since then she has had four jobs, and has returned to college and received her Ph.D. I may not have everything, but I have chosen to take bits and pieces from opportunities given to me. My mother is responsible for making these opportunities happen.

Latina women grow up thinking we can't succeed. My mother was there to tell me that this was not true. She has always lived by the saying, "Si Dios quiere." That means, "if God is willing." So far, God is willing to let my mom achieve all she is worth. To me she has never-ending value, and thanks to God she has achieved a lifetime of great accomplishments. She has helped her children lead their lives with great expectations and strong values.

In other words, why do we choose to aspire to be like the stereotypical society Latina women? Why not aspire to be an outstanding woman like my mother, who knows what a challenge is. We choose how we want to be; it does not choose us.

I open my eyes. I see my mother. She signals for me to take a picture with my brother and her at his graduation. Just the three of us is how it has been...a family with a lot of love and true emotion for each other.

La Quinceañera

Alma Garcia

As she looked on at her daughter posing for her portrait, Alma had to fight back the tears.

"Oh Mother," she could imagine Esther saying if she saw the tears. "Ya lo sabia, Mami! There go those tears, again. I knew you were going to cry."

In the dark corner in the studio, Alma waited, no longer able to fight off the tears. They filled in her eyes until they began to roll down onto her cheeks. Seeing Esther there, looking beautiful in her *quinceanera* dress, was like a dream. How could she not be proud? She could not deny that she was crying, but these were tears of joy and pride in her "nina Tete." Her thoughts raced back through the fifteen years their lives had been connected. To those times they shared with Grandpa Gerry and the emptiness they both felt when he died. To the moment Esther was born. To the memory of when those big beautiful eyes looked at her for the first time so helpless, so dependent, so confident that all would be taken care of, so at peace with the world.

It had been an adventure all right, these fifteen long years full of good times and a few not so good times, too. At times Esther showed her inner strength, the strength and determination of Queen Esther, who freed her people. It was a strength inherited from Grandma Tete who she never met, but whose name she now carried like a proud badge of honor. There were times Esther would dig in her heels and with stubborn determination, challenged a wrong because it was not right. But there were still times Esther would come and sit with her mom like she had as a small child, needing to feel safe and loved after waking from a nightmare.

There were also times, many times, when the small family would laugh together, share good times together, just Alma, Esther and Juani. There were memories of Esther being a second mom to her little sister Juani, showing her how to do things. There were the memories of the two children playing when they didn't know Alma was watching them. Esther was always making sure that Juani was safe. Esther, the little mother, looked on proudly at her little sister, making sure she learned not to let people take advantage of her generous and giving heart. She was ready to defend Juani from harm, and quick to question her about her classmates, lest Juani start going "boy crazy," too soon.

There had been times when Alma wasn't sure if this day would ever come. It had been a faraway dream, but now the dream was becoming a reality. There were days that Esther, her daughter, wasn't sure if she even wanted this *fiesta*. She knew there wasn't money to spend on extras and couldn't imagine how her mom would ever pay for everything. But Alma kept planning and saving to find a way. She knew there were no other resources, but herself to make it happen.

The lights flashed and brought Alma back to this day of celebration. There had been so many who thought this was all a big waste of time and money. And there were those who felt it was an old custom for putting a daughter on the marriage block to be bought by the highest bidder, the most successful candidate to secure her and the parents future. Alma had seen the angry and sometime passionate exchanges on the topic between fathers on either side of the pro/con discussion on quinceañeras. She also had *her* memories of *her* own quinceañera, and in the end, the *pricelessness* of the memories won out over these words spoken by men who didn't understand the '*ilusiones de una quinceañera*."

One more time the lights flashed. The session was over, but the memories were only now beginning. Alma quickly wiped her tears from her eyes. Esther walked toward her, those big beautiful eyes looking at her Mom, no longer helpless, no longer dependent for everything, just confident and strong.

Strength of Sixth Sense

Alicia Alvarez

We loved the rides at Riverview Amusement Park in Chicago, and one of our favorites was the ride across the park mid-air in gondolas. As we approached the tall and steep stairwell, I began to feel amazingly frightened. I cried and kicked, which was very out of character for me. I reluctantly went up these stairs with my mom pulling my hand and telling me how ashamed she was of my behavior. It was the most horrible feeling. I didn't recognize it; a combination of fear and a sense of a fierce fall that made my tummy feel as though an elevator bank had missed a floor!

As we approached the final step to the platform for a roundtrip sky ride across the park, I became frightened. Every time my little brother would want to get up to lean on the door and look over, I would SCREEAAM! I went into a major panic. Mom would tell my brother to sit down and behave because he was worrying his sister. About halfway across, the park officials announced that one of the gondola's doors was opened. As we approached the platform to complete half of the trip, our door automatically opened. Our door was never secured. If my brother had leaned on that door, he would have fallen out in mid air! That sense of fear and premonition saved his life. We never completed that roundtrip ride across the park, and my mom never questioned my sixth sense again.

Un Poquito Mas

A Little More

There is always room for a little more. It is a wonderful part of our nature. More fun, more love, more family, more food, whatever! With our joy and appreciation of life, we are open to experience "un poquito mas."

"Cinderella y Su Silla"
Josie B. Vasquez

It's been a year now since Dad passed away. I am still pretending that he's just away, temporarily. No se porque. I don't know why, but it's been left up to me and I've finally resigned myself to do it, to go through these photos he left for us, sus hijas y hijos. He meant for us to have them so we would have a bit of our family history to share with the grandkids, the great grandkids and the rest of la familia Banda. There are so many photos. Some I didn't even know he kept over the years, like those of us as babies, as just kids, our problem years (ha, ha) as teenagers, pictures of us with our husbands and wives (some now ex-husbands, and ex-wives), our kids, lots of kids, all the weddings, baptismals, birthday parties, Christmases, and Easter egg hunts, with us chasing each other with cascarones trying to break them over each other's heads. There were so many happy times on every occasion you could think of that familias get together to celebrate.

There are even pictures of our uncles, aunts, cousins, and us as little kids working in the fields con Ama y Apa. He even had some photos of us bathing in the creek because we didn't have indoor plumbing when we were working in the fields. Boy do those pictures bring back memories.

As I look at each picture, Dad seems so much closer than ever to me. I just feel his presence around me and can still hear his voice saying to me, "Mija, no me hablas en Ingles, como van aprender tus hijos." I laugh and he laughs with me as I struggle to speak to him in my broken Spanish. I sit back and look at these pictures of each of us and wonder with amazement at how he raised us, six kids, on his own from the time I was seven years old when my parents divorced. He couldn't even read or write and to top it off, he was color-blind.

I laugh now thinking about all the blue dresses he used to buy my older sister, Linda and me. That was the only color he really could identify easily. I'm just glad it wasn't purple or orange, or even yellow. Now that really would have been embarrassing.

Dad was usually very strict with us, the girls that is! But looking back at the sacrifices he made for each of us, especially me, the youngest girl, I now understand why he was the way he was. I have two daughters of my own now and I have found out that being the parent isn't always easy. Over protectiveness just comes naturally when you have daughters.

As I start sorting the pictures and making a pile for each of my brothers and sisters, I come across a picture of myself that takes me back to when I was a teenager, so many, many years ago, when it seemed that everything was a crisis and that I would just about die of embarrassment at the slightest thing. I see before me this young girl of fifteen years of age, looking so regal and serious, and surprisingly pretty (without my glasses, of course). Now, thinking back, I laugh to myself. This black and white picture of me was taken at the beginning of an evening that was supposed to have been my Cinderella night of all nights. Just then my oldest daughter, Belinda, walks in and asks me what I was laughing about. I show her the picture and say, "Take a guess who this is?" She looks and looks, and she can't tell it's me, her mother.

"Mija, I know you think I sometimes don't understand what you go through with school, your friends, boyfriends, that I can't relate. Let me tell you a little story about my Cinderella night which became my most embarrassing moment." The night of "Cinderella y Su Silla!"

I was very awkward as teenagers usually are at fifteen. I wore glasses, the kind from Texas State Optical that look like the Cat Woman from Batman, not the new one, but the one in the early 60's TV shows. To top it off, I was very studious. I was a bookworm, or as you might call them, a Nerd. And if that was not enough, I had a very pretty and popular older sister that I was always competing with and always losing to.

Here I was a freshman in high school. It was a new beginning in a new school, and it was going to be my year, so I thought. I had begged and begged my Daddy to let me join the drill team, which he did, with the condition that I pay for everything I needed. So, I got a part-time job on weekends at the local TG&Y five & dime store.

I was determined to be on the drill team and I made it, too! I even got my first official boyfriend, though Daddy didn't know that! Hijole, if he did I would have been in big trouble. Remember, Daddy was strict. He wouldn't even let me wear shorts outside the house or wear lipstick, let alone have a boyfriend!

Well back to this plan I had of making a name for myself in high school! This first official boyfriend was "Carlos" and boy could he dance. He was popular, he was cute, or anyway I thought he was, and the most important thing was that he was a junior upper classman! A big shot! We had been talking and walking and hugging and so on, for a few months when he asked me to go with him and his parents to the Black and White Ball. You've got to understand, the Black and White Ball was one of the most prestigious events in the community. Only the elite were invited to attend this ball. You've got to remember, I wasn't exposed to a lot of things outside of West Dallas. Back then, this was a big deal to me! This was the first formal black tie affair I had ever been invited to attend! Apa just had to let me go!

I begged and begged, and it worked again! Daddy really had a soft spot when it came to me, though I didn't realize how much until I was grown. But being that we didn't have much money to spend on extras, we just survived as best we could with what Daddy made as a bus boy at the Statler Hilton Hotel. We surely couldn't buy a new dress.

Well Carlos was determined that I would go with him, so he asked a friend of his, who just happened to be my size, if she had a dress that I could borrow for the night. Thank God for Janis. Not only did she have a dress, but she also had those long white gloves that go all the way up to your elbow to wear with it. Oh, I forgot to mention, it also had to be black or white, or black and white. That is the whole reason it's called the Black and White Ball.

I remember the day Carlos brought the dress to my house for me to try on. It was beautiful, a solid white strapless gown of lace with hoops that made it poof out like one of those southern bells. I put it on and I really felt like Cinderella going to the ball. Everything was going as planned!

Although, I had to practice with that dress, those hoops can really be a problem. Everyday for two weeks, I would rush home and put that dress on, with the large hoops underneath, and practice walking, sitting and standing. You name it; I did it. I would sit, the dress would pop up. I would lean against a wall, it would pop up again. I thought I would never get it down and manage to maneuver it under a table, but I was determined!

When the night of the ball finally came, I had my hair just right. I took off my glasses because I really didn't expect to be reading and I didn't drive yet, so I felt I could do without them! I wasn't exactly blind! You should have seen the look on my daddy's face when he saw me in that dress and wearing a white shawl with matching long gloves all ready to go to the ball. That's when this picture of me was taken. Little did I know what the night had in store for me.

When Carlos and I walked into the ballroom at the Sheraton Hotel downtown, I was in awe of all the crystal chandeliers, the beautiful decorations, and all the beautiful dresses that everyone was wearing. I had to pinch myself to make sure I wasn't dreaming and that this was for real! I now knew what it felt like to be Cinderella at the ball with my Prince Charming. It couldn't get better than this. So far, I had been able to maneuver the dress with its hoops. I had handled it in the car and as we sat at our table at one of the far corners of the ballroom. Our table was quite a distance from the dance floor, but that didn't matter to me, just being at the ball was a dream come true. The only thing missing from this dream night was to dance with my Prince Charming, but I knew that would not be a problem since Carlos was always interested in dancing.

When the band comenso con una polka, Carlos was ready to dance. He even pulled out my chair. Now that's what you call a gentleman. I've never had anyone do that for me before. As I stood up, I was ever so careful about the dress and maneuvering the hoops. Remember, it wasn't mine; I was just borrowing it for the night. Carlos, being the gentleman he was, took my hand and began to lead me through the crowded tables and chairs to get to the dance floor, while I tried to maneuver with my dress. He suddenly stopped, turned to me and said, "Do you hear something?"

"No, I don't hear anything but the music."

He took a few more steps toward the dance floor when he suddenly turned again and said, "Do you hear something dragging?"

I just shook my head, no.

He came around behind me and started to look around. Then suddenly he said, "That's it!" He proceeded to pick up the back fold of my dress's hoop and, to my embarrassment, there was a chair stuck under my dress that had gotten caught by the hoops. I had been dragging that stupid chair along with me probably since we left our table.

You cannot imagine how embarrassed I was. Here was my Prince Charming pulling a chair out from under my dress, like pulling a conejo out of a hat. The people that were crowded around at their tables couldn't help but see what was happening and they were trying not to laugh, but then my so-called Prince Charming said, "Were you trying to save your chair?" That was it. I guess he was just trying to make light of it so I wouldn't feel bad. It didn't work. The night was ruined. I just wanted to crawl up and die right then and there. Somehow, we finally made it to the dance floor, but I just couldn't forget about that chair and I kept messing up and stepping on his toes. He finally had enough and led me off the dance floor. This time though, he took the long way around so as to avoid going through the crowded tables and chairs. By the time we finally made it back to the table and I again had to maneuver my dress hoops as I sat down, I heard Carlos laughingly say to his dad, "Falta otra silla, la otra esta perdido." I knew then that I was back to being a pumpkin again. Apa never knew what happened that night. I was just too embarrassed to ever talk about it to anyone, but here I am more than thirty-five years later and I can remember that night like it was yesterday.

By this time, Belinda and I are just rolling on the floor laughing so hard the tears are streaming down our faces just imagining what all those people must have thought as they watched Carlos pulling that chair out from under my dress. When my youngest daughter, Laura, steps out of her room to see what's going on, all either one of us can do is hold up the picture as we try to explain what we're laughing about. But it's no use. We can't stop laughing.

Now I know why Dad kept all those fotos y recuerdos de la familia. It's those precious moments, those memories of growing up, as well as the growing pains we went through, that made us who we are now, and that reminds us de donde venemos. Esos fotos y recuerdos will always be with me as will my memories de mi Apa, and I will share them, like this story of my night as "Cinderella y Su Silla," with my children and my children's children and so on and so on. Going through these pictures is much easier now than when I started.

Gracias Apa por tu cariño y los recuerdos. Tu hija, Josefina.

Pancho Claus

Betty Swinners

As I started the car and pulled out of the driveway, I stopped and made an excuse to go back in the house. I ran through the house and placed the toys under the tree, ate the cookies, drank the milk and moved the logs in the fireplace. By the time we were to return home from church, Santa Claus would have made his annual visit to our house.

On the way home, we laughed and talked about how much we hoped that this Christmas, Santa Claus would pay us a visit again. My daughter was filled with questions. "How will Santa Claus get in our house? How does he know where we live? How does he know what I want? Who is Santa Claus and where does he live?" I had told her that Santa had called me at home to request her wish list. "How did Santa Claus know your telephone number?"

For the first time in my life, I took a good look at Christmas and Santa Claus. I recalled the wonderful feeling I had discovered five years prior as I celebrated my first Christmas and discovered my very first present from Santa Claus under the tree.

As a child I knew of Santa Claus because I had heard other children talk about him and the presents he brought them, but he never stopped at our house or brought me presents because my family of origin never celebrated the holidays. I did not want to lie to my ten-year-old daughter and tell her the age-old story of Santa Claus and have kids make fun of her at school, but I certainly did not want to tell her there is no Santa Claus. I chose to explain to her about the spirit of Santa Claus that I have grown to know and love. I looked into her beautiful little brown eyes filled with curiosity, excitement and Santa Claus. That's right...Santa Claus!

I explained that people are Santa Claus. Santa Claus does not live at the North Pole, have a sleigh or reindeer. Santa Claus is not an old man with a big white beard in a red suit. Santa Claus is the spirit of Christmas, the spirit of giving and kindness. Santa Claus is the wonderful feeling many people get during the holidays, regardless of whether you celebrate Hanukkah, Kwaanza, or Christmas. It is the feeling that allows families to be together and believe in the spirit of the season. Many people express their holiday spirit by putting up trees, lights and giving gifts. Others celebrate their faith in the birth of Jesus, believed to be the Son of God. With his birth, he brought faith and love.

When are you too old for Santa Claus? When you stop believing! I discovered Santa Claus at the age of twenty-five. The spirit of Santa Claus is in all people who believe, show love, and are kind. This Christmas my family and I will be waiting with excitement for Santa Claus, or Pancho Claus as I so culturally choose to name him, and as long you believe in the spirit of Santa Claus, or in our case Pancho Claus, he will always stop at your house.

Beyond Time

Maria Palacios

The women in my family
have always been the stronger gender,
the broken mold of traditional values,
Cursed by society,
envied by those
who wouldn't dare speak up,
say no,
grow wings, when flying was not something
women should do.
Daughters, sisters, mothers
nurturers, breadwinners,
female warriors of life
whose hands knew nothing
about manicures
but could silently speak
of clothes lines
and cotton fields
while making breakfast for six
with just two eggs
because they'd rather perform miracles
than wait for another empty promise
from the men who bought beer
instead of shoes for their children.
The women from my past
were soldiers in skirts
who fought against the enemy
that claimed to love them

But used the built-in weapon
between their legs
to feel superior.
I am a modern extension
of these miracle workers,
warrior of a new era
fighting the same war
I am the daughter, sister, mother,
nurturer, breadwinner
who carries the torch
of a movement, a revolution,
a proclamation of freedom,
a declaration of survival.

Kids and Their Perfect Spanish

Eddie Reyes

One day after school, while in the second grade, my niece, Rosita, came home and asked her mom, my sister Irene, "What kind of Hispanic name is B-2?" My sister asked her to repeat it and again she said that in her class was a little Hispanic boy and the teacher kept calling him B-2. My niece insisted it had to be his correct name because the little boy responded to it when the Anglo teacher called it out. After a lengthy and trying time of attempting to convince my niece that there was no such Hispanic name, my sister finally asked my niece to spell the name. My niece said, "B-2 spelled B-E-T-O!"

Year later, my same niece, Rosita, while in the eighth grade and extremely proud of her limited Spanish, was entertaining an exchange student from Mexico. Rosita decided that she would take her to IHOP for breakfast, as her guest had never been to an IHOP. As they were reviewing the menu, her guest was equally proud of her limited English, so she began to read the menu to Rosita. Although she could successfully read off the menu items with little help, she didn't always know what the item was. So, when she got to "Pigs in a Blanket," she paused for a moment with a puzzled look on her face and asked Rosita what that was. Without missing a beat and with full assertiveness, she responded, "You know...marranos en las cobijas!"

One day, while the family was in a hurry to get to church, my young nephew, Jesse, asked his mother, my sister Irene, what he should wear. She said, "Wear your pantalones de panita."

He asked, "Pantalones de – what?"

My sister responded, "de panita!"

Before my sister had a chance to say "velvet pants," his younger sister, Rosita, the Spanish-speaking expert in the family, quickly interjected with full authority and confidence, "Jesse, you know, panita...bread!"

Contributing Writers

Maricela Aguilar and her son **Alex** are natives of Dallas. She is a community leader who takes the initiative in issues and causes which positively impact Latinos. He is a young Latino leader in the making. She credits her family for her civic involvement.

Alex Alaniz is currently an executive manager for a large corporation in Chicago, Illinois. Alex received his Bachelor's degree in Marketing from Northern Illinois University.

Elena Alaniz is currently a bilingual teacher in Aurora, Illinois. She enjoys giving back to her community by teaching and assuring young Latino students that they can succeed.

Alicia Maria Alvarez is a community activitist, orguillosa mujer Latina Americana, native of Illinois, transplanted to Texas for twenty-two years, where her heart remains to this day!

Milena Canal's greatest blessing is being the mother of two beautiful children. She is a realtor who resides in Houston, Texas.

E. B. Castro Jr., is a gifted florist and businessman. His store, *The Rose Shop*, has provided San Antonio with unparalleled beauty and service for over seventy-five years.

Ellen Castro is a best-selling author. She holds an EdM from Harvard and an MBA from SMU where she currently serves on the faculty of the Business Leadership Center. In addition to Ellen's writings, speaking, teaching and consulting, she is a realtor.

Eloise Castro is a native and resident of San Antonio. She is the office manager for the prestigious *Rose Shop*. Eloise has a talented son, Allen. Her other joy is "Max," a charismatic Pekinese.

Raoul Lowery Contreras is one of the longest published Hispanic essayist and Op-Ed writers in the USA. He has been published weekly since 1988. Over 1,000 articles and four books have been written by Contreras. A native of Mexico City, he lives in San Diego, California.

Lupe A. Davila is a veteran realtor in The Woodlands, Texas, in partnership with her husband Roger. Roger and Lupe have two grown children and are the grandparents of two grandsons who reside in Boston.

Roxanne Del Rio has pursued a twenty-year career in management education, recruiting worldwide. Her interests focus on educational issues in socially diverse societies. She has championed Hispanic advancement at a boardroom level as well as through grass-roots initiatives.

Sylvia Fuentes received her Doctorate in Adult Continuing Education. She is currently the Director of the Latino Resource Center at Northern Illinois University.

Alma Garcia lives in Oakland, California, with her daughter Juana. A graduate of Mills College, she is currently the Library Systems Administrator for the F.W. Olin Library.

Enriqueta Garrett was born in La Habana, Cuba. She immigrated to the US at age twelve. She is a Dallas' Adamson high school graduate with a BBA from UTA. She is also the proud mother of William Tomas Garrett.

Gilda Garza is the first Hispanic female elected to the McKinney, Texas city council, She is also a charter member of The League of United Latin American Citizens (LULAC), revitalized Council #608 (first female president, 2001).

Minerva Gorena, EdD., is senior advisor to the National Clearinghouse for English Language Acquisition (NCELA) at The George Washington University in Washington, DC.

Verónica Guajardo, is a writer and musician that lives in the barrio of Southside Modesto, California's Central Valley. She is part of the Rudo Revolutionary Front (as Kika Ruda), a collective of poets, actors, musicians and hip-hop artists.

Alida Hernandez has thirty-eight years of professional experience in meeting the employment needs of individuals and businesses. She also worked for over thirty years with community-oriented non-profits, utilizing her expertise in providing leadership in fundraising efforts.

Rita Urias Mendoza is from a Southern California farm labor family. Rita and her late husband, Modesto, raised five children in Oxnard, California where she resides.

Maria R. Palacios is a poet, activist, performer and Polio survivor who uses poetry to inspire and empower women. Maria R. Palacios is the founder of Atahualpa Press and author of a book of poems, *The Female King*, an inspirational collection of prose and poetry, such as *Karate on Wheels, A Journey of Self Discovery*.

Teresa Perez has held positions in school and work as news editor and/or writer for internal publications. She holds degrees from the University of Texas in Austin and Texas State University. She is a member of the Hispanic Women's Network of Texas and National Society of Hispanic MBAs.

Eva Rangel is the manager for the Nueva Vida Transitional Supportive Counseling Program of Women

Together/Mujeres Unidas. She is one of the founders of the Latina Task Force of The Texas Council on Family.

Eddie Reyes is a disabled Vietnam Veteran, a former Dallas Police Officer, a successful entrepreneur and has adopted four teenage Hispanic young ladies at the same time.

Betty Ramirez Swinners has dedicated her life to sharing her story of success and survival to encourage others to believe in themselves. She is the Owner/CEO of Diversity Speakers.

Josie B. Vasquez is a second generation Texan, the sixth in a family of nine children. She's currently a consultant specializing in workplace discrimination issues.

Maria Reyes Velasco is a firm believer in "ancestral memory." Her pen name is "la michicana" which comes from Los Mechicas, Michigan & Chicana. Honoring her ancestors and listening to her "singing heart" inspires her.

If you have enjoyed "Tortilla Soup for the Spirit" and would like to order additional copies you can order from

www.outskirtspress.com/tortillasoup

Additionally, for more information or to request a speaking engagement or other services, please contact:

Ellen Castro
www.ellencastro.com
TEL: 214.750.7718
ellen@ellencastro.com
P.O. Box 12188
Dallas, TX 75225
USA

Betty Ramirez Swinners
www.diversityspeakers.com
TEL: 972-864-5516
betty@diversityspeakers.com
PO Box 181393
Dallas, Texas 75043
USA

Printed in the United States
50690LVS00002B/7-15

9 781598 002119